MIND AND BELIEF:
PSYCHOLOGICAL ASCRIPTION
AND THE CONCEPT OF BELIEF

MIND AND BELIEF:

PSYCHOLOGICAL ASCRIPTION AND THE CONCEPT OF BELIEF

by

MITCHELL GINSBERG

London

GEORGE ALLEN AND UNWIN LTD

RUSKIN HOUSE   MUSEUM STREET

FIRST PUBLISHED IN GREAT BRITAIN IN 1972

ISBN number, 004-100-032-3

To

Solomon from Krasnoyarsk

and

Simon from Bari

PREFACE

This work is the present statement of considerations which in a former incarnation functioned as my doctoral thesis. The thesis was formally presented to the Department of Philosophy of the University of Michigan in early September 1967. Since then it has served in one or another form as the major text for a seminar in philosophical psychology primarily for Philosophy majors at Yale University. It underwent its last major transformation from a pile to a type-written entity in 1969 under the hands of Nancy Kaplan, to whom I owe both appreciation and thanks.

Since 1965 I have enjoyed and learned from conversations about positions held in this work with Richard Brandt, William Alston, Alvin Goldman, J. O. Urmson, Robert Solomon, Nancy Kubany Hart, Roland Pfaff, Laura McMullen Krauss, Allen Hazen, Yvonne Ginsberg, Loren Mosher, M.D., and with others. Although I assume that none of the people mentioned disagrees totally with what I say here, I am not attempting to albatross them with anything they might reject.

I have found that the project of analyzing the concept of belief and of addressing the issues to which this activity leads is such that one is continually forced to accept, at least tentatively, several positions outside of philosophical psychology itself. Since I am not always perfectly content with these positions, I have felt temptations to address questions about them. The desire and the contextual need to limit these tangential investigations have not increased my degree of contentment significantly. I think that these outriggings could be replaced with other perhaps more adequate answers to such questions generating only minor problems of reformulation of the basic lines of this work, but I will not attempt to argue for that claim here.

Indian Summer 1970
Cheshire

CONTENTS

NOTE ON PUNCTUATION

In this work, I will employ several conventions of punctuation which are common in contemporary philosophical writings. As there are various mutually incompatible philosophical conventions, and since some of these conventions are slightly at variance with certain literary traditions, I would like to make explicit which ones will be followed here.

I will use single quotation marks when talking about the word or phrase within them; e.g., when noting that the word 'belief' is a noun. A punctuation mark (e.g., a period) closing a sentence will *follow* the quotation mark of such a quoted word or phrase, as when discussing the senses of the word 'division'. When an entire sentence appears within single quotation marks, a mark of punctuation at its end signifies the intonation pattern to be used in reading the sentence; e.g., when the mark in question is a period, a declarative sentence intonation pattern. In this way, we can talk of the sentence 'He believes that God is good.' as an example of a sentence which can be used to attribute a certain belief to someone. If such a quotation occurs at the end of a sentence, a closing punctuation mark will also *follow* the closure of this type of quotation *unless* the mark in question is a period, in which case it will be omitted, as when we consider the sentence 'I believe you understand this convention.'

Double quotation marks are used to quote directly from other sources. Only what actually appears in the original source will be written within the quotation marks. Thus, if we close a sentence with a directly quoted phrase which is not followed by a period in the original text, no period will precede the closure of the quotation; e.g., in quoting some philosopher's claim that belief is a "psychic act". The only exception to this will be to allow for ellipses (three periods will signify an omission of text) and for explanatory additions (brackets will be used for this purpose).

If the quoted portion itself ends with a punctuation mark (as in the case in which an interrogative sentence is quoted in its entirety), the quotation mark will follow this terminal punctuation, and the sentence in which the quotation appears will itself be closed by the appropriate punctuation, again with the exception of a period, which I accept as redundant. Thus, have you ever heard of the claim of certain psychologists, "The infant is capable of learning within the first few hours of its postnatal life."?

The double quotation marks are also used to draw attention to extended uses or otherwise unusual uses of the word or phrase within them. As an example employing this and an earlier-stated convention for *single* quotation marks, I would hold that the word 'beliefs' is used in an extended sense when one talks of the "beliefs" of cash registers.

This distinction between single and double quotation marks is maintained within direct quotations. What appears as single (or double) quotation marks in a given text remains the same within direct quotation. If I were to quote part of the last sentence in the preceding paragraph, for example, I might talk of the individual who held "that the word 'beliefs' is used in an extended sense when one talks of the "beliefs" of cash registers." Note that here I differ slightly from the most usual literary convention.

INTRODUCTION

This work is not in the philosophy of religion. Basically, it concerns questions in philosophical psychology, and in particular, questions both about what it is to hold something to be the case (to believe something), and also about attributing various psychological characteristics to given individuals (human beings, etc.) and about to which beings such ascriptions are appropriate. Since the words 'belief', 'believe', etc. are perhaps slightly misleading on this matter when considered out of context, let me in this brief introduction say what I will be talking about on the pages which follow.

The word 'belief' and its cognates come closest in English to allowing for an accurate demarcation of the major topic of this work's first part. One major problem with this family of words is that it suggests to some that the topic is limited to instances (to beliefs) of great importance. Accordingly, one might expect talk only of the belief in God, the belief that one's nation is taking an essentially correct course of action on some issue, the belief that one should treat all fellow living creatures kindly, etc.

I would like to state explicitly that I do not so intend to limit the topic at hand. I want to include as beliefs what others might consider to be too trivial to count as beliefs, such as the belief that the sun is shining, that a certain person's name is Laura, that a bachelor is a bachelor, etc. In virtue of this, one might suggest replacement of talk of one who believes something with talk of one who thinks something and of one who is of some opinion. This *is* rather appealing insofar as it seems to help eliminate confusion about one major topic of this work. Talk of thoughts and of opinions, that is, is preferable to talk of beliefs in that it does not carry with it implications of gravity, yet there are reasons for which I have not opted for either talk of thoughts or of opinions.

First, 'thought' is a word with many meanings—*The Random*

House Dictionary of the English Language giving twelve separately numbered entries for 'thought'—one of which is 'opinion', but others which are as diverse as 'judgment', 'concept', 'intellectual activity', and 'faculty of reasoning'—and twenty-six for 'think', including 'believe', 'suppose', 'conceive in the mind', and 'ponder'. I have decided to avoid the problem of having to distinguish the appropriate sense of 'think' and of 'thought' from all the others by talking of believing and of beliefs and not of thinking and of thoughts.

Second, 'opinion' has as a fault the fact that it suggests the excluding of instances (of opinions, of beliefs) of which the possessor is completely convinced and for which he has excellent grounds. (Consistent with the preceding remarks about 'belief', I would, if I *were* to make use of the word 'opinion', like not to limit its scope in this way.) More importantly, the related verb is 'opine'. I would prefer to use 'believe', partly because the latter is much more deeply entrenched in my idiolect and partly because 'opine' is ambiguously equivalent to 'have an opinion' ('be of the opinion'), to 'express a belief', to 'judge', and to 'state'. I will want to make a clear distinction between these. See the text itself for more detailed discussion.

MIND AND BELIEF:
PSYCHOLOGICAL ASCRIPTION
AND THE CONCEPT OF BELIEF

CHAPTER I

THE CONCEPT OF BELIEF

This chapter will give an account of what beliefs are. In the course of this presentation I will review some of the earlier attempts to explicate the notion of belief, but this will be done primarily as a way of giving a contrast against which my positive suggestions can stand out.

Although philosophers have written much on the notion of belief, i.e., on what a belief is, they have agreed to little beyond its being something mental. Of course to attribute a belief to some individual is to presuppose that this individual is the *sort* of thing which *can* have beliefs. As I will have occasion to talk of such a being, and there is no precedent use of some technical term for this purpose, I will hereinafter refer to any entity which has a mind and therefore *can* have beliefs (and also wants, emotions, etc.) as a mind-possessor, or, in short, an MP.

Philosophers have claimed, then, that to attribute a belief to some entity (to an MP) is to claim that it possesses some mental "something", that it has some mental characteristic, etc. But this type of claim is rather unenlightening unless we attempt to explicate these notions. Rather than spending more time here trying to formulate some position consistent with the many analyses of belief in western philosophy, however, let us consider some rather detailed, but nonetheless inadequate, suggestions made in the literature.

It has been held by several philosophers, most prominently Hume, that a belief is something given or presented to the consciousness of an MP, much as a sensation or a mental picture.

In this work I will not make use of the contemporary notion of sense data. One of the major reasons for this is that I wish to avoid the problems which might arise because of readers' different preconceptions about precisely what sense data are.[1] In addition, I would like to avoid certain specific problems supposedly inherent in this notion, such as its involving (a) the postulation of an epistemologically superfluous entity, viz., the sense datum, and, (b) a confusion about the epistemological status of physical objects. (For an extended example of the presentation of such problems, see J. L. Austin's *Sense and Sensibilia*.[2]) Without resting what I have to say on any particular theory of knowledge, I would like to introduce the notion of a phenomenologically presented entity, or, in short, of a PPE. This notion can be explicated once we introduce the notion of the phenomenological field. This latter notion is modelled on that of the visual field. One's phenomenological field is one's entire perceptual field, or in other words, one's consciousness. Correlatively, we may introduce PPEs as member contents of consciousness. What will count as examples of PPEs depends on one's theory of knowledge (cf. the close of footnote 28), but accepting both typically undisputed examples such as sensations and also sometimes disputed examples such as (*some*) spatiotemporal entities, *both for the sake of example*, we could give as examples of PPEs: sensations, twitches, pains, cramps, aches, the taste of sugar or salt or gouda cheese or a bordeaux wine, the sight of wheat waving in a field, the smell of fine perfume, particular tokens of bits of language such as words, both audible (e.g., as spoken by others) and visible (e.g., as seen on a printed page, or as imagined in a dark room with one's eyes closed), and the whining of a siren. Other examples could easily be presented.

Hume, and others, then, are suggesting that a belief is a PPE. This claim can be filled out in various ways. Hume himself suggested at least two different, although mutually inconsistent, characterizations of belief. Both involve rather basic

---

[1]One way to structure these different views is in terms of whether each given view holds that there is or is not a parallel or isomorphism between the sense data/non sense data distinction and each of the following distinctions: perceived/physical, internal/external, ideal/real, subjective/objective, and illusory/veridical.

[2]New York, Oxford University Press, 1964. See also the discussion in note 28 of this chapter.

misunderstandings of the concept of belief. (It will be argued below that all analyses claiming beliefs to be PPEs involve such misunderstandings.)

One holding a belief to be a PPE might hold, for example, that a belief is a mental picture (a kind of thought) which is much more vivid than any case of imagination (in which one tries to picture something he accepts as not being the case).[3] A belief, then, on this analysis, is a PPE. It is in someone's consciousness at some given time, and one can distinguish between believing something and imagining something by noting how clear the mental picture is. If it has fine detail, then it is obviously a belief, and if it does not, then it is just a case of imagination.

Or it might be held that a belief is another kind of PPE. It may be, not a mental picture itself, but rather a feeling or a sensation of agreement with the thought, i.e., with the mental picture, which accompanies the thought in one's consciousness.

In his *Treatise*, Hume claims, "An opinion, therefore, or belief may be most accurately defin'd, A LIVELY IDEA RELATED TO OR ASSOCIATED WITH A PRESENT IMPRESSION." (Book I, Part III, Sect. VII, p. 96, his capitalization.) Compare this with his discussion of the difference between fictions (e.g., cases of daydreaming, fantasizing, etc.) and beliefs in his *Inquiry*:

> The difference between *fiction* and *belief* lies in some sentiment or feeling which is annexed to the latter, not to the former, and which depends not on the will, nor can be demanded at pleasure. (Sect. 5, part 2, p. 61, his italics.)

---

[3]See D. Hume, *A Treatise of Human Nature* (Oxford, Oxford University Press, 1964), Book I, Part III, Sect. X, pp. 119-120, (his italics.) "Belief . . . is nothing but *a more vivid and intense conception of an idea.*" Cf. D. Hume, *An Inquiry Concerning Human Understanding* (New York, The Bobbs-Merrill Co., Inc., 1955), "I say that belief is nothing but a more vivid, lively, forcible, firm, steady conception of an object than what the imagination alone is ever able to attain." (Sect. 5, part 2, p. 62.)

Russell, in discussing beliefs, distinguished the having of a belief from the belief itself. He calls the former the believing and the latter the belief. He, taking a position similar to Hume's, says that "the believing is an actual experienced feeling, not something postulated . . ."[4]

In these analyses the belief is individuated, i.e., distinguished from other beliefs, by the characteristics of the thought (for Hume, the mental picture) which is relevant to the belief. Thus, the belief that one's sister is in the room is different from the belief that the fire in one's fireplace is blazing warmly, (at least partially) because the two thoughts (mental pictures, for Hume) are not identical. We add the restriction that this may provide only partial criteria for differentiation, because the two beliefs may differ also in other ways, e.g., in the degree of clarity of detail.

Here, then, are two analyses of belief as a PPE. In what ways are they inadequate? And in what ways can these inadequacies illuminate what beliefs are?

One inadequacy is that such analyses do not allow for unconscious beliefs. I take it that something is an unconscious characteristic of an MP if (a) it is a psychological characteristic, (b) the MP honestly (earnestly) asserts that he does not have that characteristic (e.g., of wanting to castrate his father), and (c) in fact he does have that characteristic. I want to maintain below, however, that it is possible for someone to have a belief, for him to avow earnestly that he does not have that belief, and for him to be mistaken (but not deceitful) in his avowal.

In order to show the plausibility of claiming that there are unconscious beliefs, let us consider the following case of post-hypnotic suggestion. The hypnotist tells the subject under hypnosis that upon awakening he will remember nothing of what happened while he was hypnotized, but will stand as soon as the hypnotist lights a cigarette, and will remain standing until

---

[4]*The Analysis of Mind* (London, George Allen & Unwin, Ltd., 1924), p. 233.

the cigarette is extinguished. The subject is then brought out of
the trance, recalls nothing of what happened under hypnosis,
and stands for the period during which the hypnotist has a
cigarette lit. The subject explains this behavior in terms of his *him*.
feeling nervous, fidgety, etc., but *not* in terms of his wanting to
obey the hypnotist and believing that the hypnotist told him
to stand while he (the hypnotist) has a cigarette lit. Insofar as
we can explain his post-hypnotic behavior by attributing the
above-stated desire and belief to him, and yet admit that the
person does not realize that these are correct ascriptions, we
have reason to attribute this (unconscious) belief (as well as
this unconscious desire) to him.[5]

I think that the possibility of unconscious beliefs *is* a problem for such an analysis of belief, but I feel that there is
another problem—a completely unresolvable dilemma. For if a
belief is analyzed as something given in one's phenomenological
field, in one's consciousness, then one has a belief only so long
as this PPE is in one's phenomenological field. (The following
criticism will also handle the closely related analysis of belief
in which the belief is not the PPE, but a relation which obtains
between the PPE in question and the person.)

Given (as an additional but not radical assumption) that
one does not have at any one time an indefinitely large number
of thoughts that one is thinking (either as a silent monologue or
as, in accordance with Hume's analysis of thinking, the having
of mental pictures), then we are forced to conclude that one
has very few beliefs at any given time. This is an extremely
unacceptable implication of the Humean analysis, and, in
general, of any analysis taking a belief to be a PPE.

It also follows that as soon as one stops thinking about something (as soon as the thought leaves one's consciousness), one
no longer has the belief in question. In addition, it must then
be claimed that a person who is asleep but is not dreaming (i.e.,

---

[5]This case is taken from T. X Barber, "Hypnosis as Perceptual-Cognitive
Restructuring: II. "Post"-Hypnotic Behavior," *Journal of Clinical and
Experimental Hypnosis,* vol. 6 (1958), pp. 10-20, esp. pp. 11-12.

one who has no thoughts at all at that moment) must be said to have *no* beliefs at all at that time. But then no one is a devout theist in his dreamless sleep, and people are almost continually completely changing their beliefs (as fast as they change what they're thinking!)

Notice that my criticisms do not rely on Hume's presuppositions about the nature of thinking, viz., that thinking is like having a movie being played on one's mental "screen" (consciousness), but only on that aspect of his analyses which equates belief to a mental happening or occurrence, or more exactly, to something which is presented in such an occurence (of thinking), i.e. to a PPE. The criticisms are thus independent of which analysis of thinking we should find adequate on other grounds.

Hume's analyses are clearly inadequate. Rather than embarking on an extended discussion about what (philosophical reasons) might lead one to give such answers to the question of what beliefs are, we shall limit ourselves here to noting that we might explain how one might come to the Humean position in the following way. This explanation should be considered as a reconstruction which makes intelligible how one might have come to the Humean position. It is *not* intended to be a historically correct explanation of how Hume himself arrived at his position.

One can begin the analysis of what beliefs are by considering the question of how one makes the judgment at a certain time that he has a given belief. If one has an answer to this question and also does not distinguish clearly between this question and that of what it is for someone to have a given belief, one might assume that the answer to the first question is also an adequate answer to the second.

One might, then, give a Humean analysis of the question of (1) how anyone goes about judging that he has a given belief. This analysis, if then proposed as one's answer to the related but distinguishable question of (2) what it is to have a belief, would essentially be Hume's position on what beliefs are.

We have shown, however, that beliefs are not PPEs. In coming to the conclusion that a belief is not a PPE, we have forced the retraction of a very simple explanation of an obvious fact: that when asked whether or not we have a given belief, in an indefinitely large number of cases we answer immediately and with great assurance, and in a large portion of such cases we are correct in our answer. But we can no longer explain this fact by saying that what one does here is have the thought (which *is* the given belief) in one's consciousness, and examine it for the characteristics upon which one could base one's claim. We cannot say that we have the given belief because we have "seen" it (in our consciousness) for the reason that it is not the kind of thing which can be (perceived) in consciousness. This is not to say that there is *nothing* presented to consciousness which can be interestingly related to some certain belief, but simply that what is in such a case presented to consciousness is not the belief itself. We will discuss this in more detail below, in distinguishing between beliefs and judgments.

We will not explain this fact (viz., that one can so quickly and accurately state whether he has a given belief or not) in this chapter, but will merely note here that this explanatory power is one of the desirable characteristics for a theory of belief to have. (See chapter II.) It is because of this that one who rejects a purely Humean analysis of belief might nonetheless want to say that there is *some* phenomenological element in beliefs. (This is *not* intended to be a historically correct explanation of the genesis of any of the positions to be discussed below.)

We have, for example, the suggestion that to attribute a belief to a person (or in general, to an MP) is to make two claims in one. It is to assert, first of all, that the person contemplates or "entertains" the belief in question (and perhaps also judges that he does in fact have that belief) and, secondly, is disposed to act in a way appropriate to the truth of the belief in question.

That is, it is claimed that having a belief is actually both having certain PPEs and also having dispositions to certain behavior. Thus, R. B. Braithwaite claims that "a belief in p consists in entertaining p and being disposed to act appropriately to p's being true."[6]

Such analyses have several formulations, but rather than discuss them separately, we can consider the position in its most general formulation. Half of having a belief, then, is having thought about it at some time. (Different species of this analysis will take different positions on the questions of (a) whether one has the belief only at those times when one is considering the belief, or also at those times subsequent to when the MP in question has considered the belief, and of (b) whether one must also "nod agreement internally" with the belief, that is, whether one must conclude, at the time at which he thinks about the belief p, that p is true.) The other half of having a belief is having a disposition to act appropriately to the belief's being true.

Let us consider these two halves separately. If having a belief (conceptually) requires having considered the belief at some time (whether at the time for which the belief is being ascribed to the MP, or at some prior time), then we are in a position to explain why it is that we would refuse to ascribe an anachronistic belief to an MP. We would reject, for example, *both* the claim that Rembrandt believed that Andy Warhol is a great artist and a genius *and also* the claim that Rembrandt believed that Andy Warhol is not a great artist and genius. On this theory, this can be explained by noting that Rembrandt never heard of Mr. Warhol at all. (From this it follows that Rembrandt had *no* beliefs concerning Warhol's talent or lack of talent.)

But another consequence of such an analysis of belief is not quite so acceptable. We have a friend, for example, who finds that she is very uneasy every time she visits her home town of Detroit, that she becomes depressed there, etc. When she returns to her new home in New York City and meets many friends that she has known before, she is quite happy. She realizes that there are many more people that she can com-

---

[6]"The Nature of Believing," *Proceedings of the Aristotelian Society*, vol. 33 (1932-33), pp. 114-145.

municate with in New York than in Detroit. Furthermore, she
also knows that her husband can advance his career in New
York but that Detroit would be stifling to him. At this point,
we may be willing to ascribe the belief to her that it is
better for her and her husband to live in New York City than
in Detroit. But this is so even if, for example, we are given
the information that she *never* either said to herself 'It's better
for us to live in New York City than in Detroit.' or asked herself
'Is it better for us to live in New York City than in Detroit?'
Stated more theoretically, we do *not* hold it as a disproof of
her having the belief in question, p, that she never questioned
whether p was true or not or considered the possibility of her
having that belief.

Or, stated more generally, it is *not* required for the correct
ascription of a belief to an MP that he have considered the
belief either at some time prior to or at the time at which it is
the case that he has that belief.

But since that is so, the first half of the analysis of belief
being considered is inadequate, and therefore, the analysis
must be rejected. Before we do this, however, let us consider
the second half (viz., having a disposition to act appropriately
to the belief's being true) to see if we can thereby gain some
insight into the nature of believing.

I suppose that what philosophers who advance this thesis
are taking "acting appropriately to the belief's being true" to
consist of is either acting as if the belief *were* true, or acting as
if the MP *knew* that the belief is true.

If we consider the first alternative, it follows from this
analysis that one can be said to believe that p (where 'p' is
to be replaced by the statement of the belief in question)
only if one has a disposition to act as if the belief were true.

We can look at the following case. Someone believes, for
example, that he is the heir to his country's throne. He also
believes, however, that if he does anything whatsoever to
inform *anyone* of his identity, to make known his rights, to
try to ascend to the throne, etc., etc., anti-royalists who are
keeping close watch over him will quickly end his life. We

add that he loves living and is content in his present situation, and in addition is a coward. We now have a case in which this person had no disposition to act as if it were true that he is the heir to his country's throne, in spite of the fact that he has this belief.

It might be argued at this point that one cannot (agreeing with our position) analyze believing that p as having a disposition to act as if p were true, *but* that such a dispositional analysis *will* succeed when analyzing all of one's beliefs. Such an analysis would claim that believing that S, where S is the set of all of one's beliefs, is having a disposition to act as if S were true.

Even if such an analysis were correct, it would face the following problem. We are in search of a position which will allow us to generate analyses of individual beliefs. We want to be able to analyze what believing p amounts to without having to ask the question of what believing p and q and r etc. amounts to. This reflects the intuition that believing p is believing p no matter what other beliefs are held. The analysis of an entire set of beliefs does not, however, allow us to continue to the analysis of members of that set. An analysis of individual beliefs, however, *will* allow us to continue to the analysis of the set.

But in addition to this problem, the analysis of such a set of beliefs as the disposition to act as if all of the members of that set were true is unacceptable.

To see why this is so, let us consider the following. We can use a simplified case of one having only one belief. Our case is the following. Ken believes that (a) he is going to attend law school next fall.[7]

---

[7]The artificiality of such examples has its difficulties. In this case, for example, it is necessary, even after the attribution to Ken of wants and personality traits, to assume that he has *some* additional beliefs, such as beliefs about what would count as his misleading others about his believing (a).

It seems that single *isolated* beliefs have no dispositions associated with them (but have some only if, inter alia, *other* beliefs are actually smuggled into the example in question).

Let us overlook the problem that it is not terribly obvious just what the disposition to act as if (a) were true amounts to. This dispositional analysis still faces the following problem: It is possible to attribute wants and personality traits to Ken such that it will then be false to say that he has the disposition to act as if (a) were true. Let us add, then, that Ken is extremely cruel, rather sadistic, and intensely wants (out of perversity) to have everyone misjudge what his (Ken's) belief is. In such a case, Ken has belief (a), but has no disposition to act as if it were true.

The general implication of this is that what disposition of the sort in question one will have depends not only on one's beliefs, but also on one's wants, personality traits, intentions, etc., and that by attributing certain of these latter to an individual with a given set of beliefs, the dispositions in question will be altered. If this is so, such a dispositional analysis of beliefs will necessarily be found faulty. This, then, provides us with a counter-example of the first interpretation of Braithwaite's analysis of belief.

We now face the second possible interpretation of the Braithwaite position. We are told that part of what is involved in having some belief is having a disposition to act *as if* one knew that the belief is true. Given, for example, that an MP believes that Italian is a much more lyrical language than German, we supposedly know that the MP has a disposition to act if he *knew* that Italian is a much more lyrical language than German.

But what does this tell us? If we can say anything about how this MP will act in this case, it is because we assume that, given that he has a disposition to act as if he knew that p, we can conclude that he has a disposition to act as if he believed that p. As far as bringing it about that we know what one is likely to do, ascriptions of knowledge are informative insofar as they entail ascriptions of belief. The additional entailment that what is believed is true is irrelevant to the question of what the MP is likely to do. In this light we can say that belief is a more purely psychological notion than is knowledge, which is partially a truth-evaluative notion (evaluates in terms of truth-value). On these grounds one might agree with Chisholm that the concept of knowledge is less obviously something purely psychological than is the concept of belief.[8] Furthermore, let us consider an implication of this interpretation of the Braithwaitean claim. It follows that one believes that p only if one is disposed to act as if he believed that p. But the above case of the heir to the throne is also a counter-example to this. We admit that he has the belief in question, but add that he has no disposition to act as if he believed it (for to do so would be to shorten his life-span considerably).

The Braithwaitean analysis, then, is unacceptable. There is an analysis of belief which is similar to that contained in the second part of the above one, but which is, however, more open than Braithwaite's claim, and might, therefore, be correct even if Braithwaite's is not. Let us consider then, the following analysis, proposed by H. H. Price. "Believing a proposition is, I think, a disposition and not an occurrence or "mental act," though the disposition is not necessarily a very long-lived one and may only last a few seconds."[9] Price leaves open just what dispositions a given belief will consist of. Whether or not a dispositional analysis of belief will be ultimately acceptable or not depends, prima facie (but see below), on how one might spell out the dispositions involved in given beliefs. The present question, then, is whether one can cite the dispositions which would adequately analyze individual beliefs. (One *can*, of course, do so only if there *are* such sets of dispositions.) For this, let us turn to a rather influential view, that of philosophical behaviorism; and, in particular, to the thought of Ryle.

Ryle's main concern in his *Concept of Mind* is to dissolve what he regards as the "myth of the ghost in the machine" (whatever that amounts to), and in his attempt at dissolving

---

[8]"Sentences about Believing," *Minnesota Studies in the Philosophy of Science,* vol. 2, (ed. H. Feigl, M. Scriven, and G. Maxwell (Minneapolis, University of Minnesota Press, 1963)), pp. 510-520.

[9]"Belief and Will," *Proceedings of the Aristotelian Society,* Supplementary Volume 28 (1954), p. 15.

the myth, Ryle suggests that beliefs are tendencies, and thus unlike knowledge, which is a capacity. Or, in the formal mode, that the word 'believe' is a tendency verb whereas 'know' is a capacity verb. (See p. 133). Thus, for Ryle, to attribute a belief to some MP is to attribute certain dispositions to him. These dispositions are, moreover, tendencies, and not capabilities.

Given this sketch of Ryle's position, then, it is time to face the question of whether beliefs can in some way be conceptually reduced to these tendencies.

Given, for example, that Eve believes that the ice is thin, what tendencies can we offer to replace the belief-ascription? Ryle suggests that to have this belief is to have the tendencies to avoid skating on the ice, to agree when others assert that the ice is thin, to object when others claim that it isn't, etc. (See pp. 133f.)

The most obvious difficulty with such a position is that it is true both that (a) one can have the belief in question without having any of the tendencies with which the belief is associable, and also that (b) one can have the tendencies with which the belief is associable without having the belief. (This is relevant to the discussion below about belief as a "cluster" of dispositions. See the last part of this discussion of Ryle's position.) To take Ryle's own example, we can see an instance of the former situation when Eve not only believes that the ice is thin but also wants to fall in or wants very much to fool everyone into thinking that she *doesn't* have this belief. Or, when she has this belief, but wants others to act on the supposition that the ice is not at all thin, (Acting as if one knew the ice to be solid is one way to bring this desired result about.)

A counter-example in which the latter situation obtains is when the MP wants others to believe that he believes that the ice is thin but he in fact does not have this belief.

The point of these counter-examples is the following: On any simple reduction of belief-ascription to tendency-ascription, we can generate counter-examples which show that the reduction is inadequate. That is, we can show that if one takes the ascription of a belief to be a "disguised" ascription of tendencies to act, to think, etc. in certain ways, we can show that there are cases where we would accept either the belief-ascription or the tendencies-ascription but *not* both.

We have shown, that is, that if Ryle suggests that having a given belief is to be analyzed as having a *set* of tendencies to act in certain ways, we can construct counter-examples in which we will accept the claim that the individual has the belief in question but will reject certain of the claims that he has the tendencies in question.

Our general method of constructing counter-examples to any Rylean claims of tendency-reduction of beliefs is to postulate that the individual has not only the belief in question (being conceptually analyzed), but also certain wants, personality traits, other beliefs, etc. such that it would be clear that in such cases it would be unacceptable to postulate certain of the tendencies given in the Rylean analysis.

If a dispositional analysis is to be adequate, then, it will have to be more sophisticated than that programatically suggested by Ryle. But even more sophisticated formulations will be inadequate because the general program of a dispositional reduction of beliefs is conceptually unacceptable.

To see this, let us consider the logical structure of a dispositional analysis. The analysis will present us with a set of disposition-or tendency-claims which supposedly analyze the claim that a certain belief is held by some MP. That is, the analysis will claim that a certain statement that some MP has a given belief means the same as the given set of statements attributing certain dispositions or tendencies to that MP.

At this point, the dispositional analysis faces the following problem: Let us suppose the set of tendencies given as analyzing a given belief consists of some large number of members, say five hundred. (Actually, each belief might perhaps be correlated with indefinitely many tendencies.) If we can generate a case in which we accept the attribution of the belief in question, but reject the attribution of just one of the tendencies in question to the MP, the dispositional analysis will thereby be shown to be incorrect.

This can be avoided only if a dispositional analysis can specify which dispositions it is logically necessary that one possess for one to possess the belief in question. But there is no one tendency such that we would be willing to reject the ascription of the belief in question, provided that we also supposed that he has a great many other dispositions held to manifest that belief. This being so, a dispositional analysis cannot do justice to the fact that attribution of beliefs is based on a complex of factors which are such that any given belief-manifestation may be absent, and yet the attribution will nonetheless be acceptable.

For example, let us for the moment assume that a belief can be explicated in this way in terms of dispositions, and that the following set of five dispositions analyzes the belief that Ryle is an excellent philosopher: (1) the disposition to read Ryle when wanting to read an insightful analysis of some philosophical concept, (2) the disposition to laud Ryle as a philosopher when being earnest, (3) the disposition to disagree with anyone who claims that Ryle is almost always philosophically myopic, (4) the disposition to go out of one's way to show how Ryle proposed short sketches of more recent analyses elaborated by others which are held to be rather penetrating analyses, and, (5) the disposition to assert that Ryle is an excellent philosopher.

If one often manifests four of these dispositions (e.g.: (1), (2), (4), and (5)) but never manifests the fifth (here: (3)), we still might very well attribute the belief in question to him. The fact that there is no reason to attribute disposition (3) here is evidence against this belief-attribution (given that we are for the moment assuming the dispositional analysis above to be adequate), but the many manifestations of the other dispositions constitute much stronger evidence *for* it. (Overwhelming evidence is overwhelming.)

Furthermore, it is in general the case that the attribution of many wants, character traits, *other* beliefs, etc., to one having the belief in question is such that *many* of the dispositions held to analyze the given belief would be denied ascription to the one involved. This has already been suggested in our discussions above of various dispositional analyses. For support for this position in the form of examples, consider the above discussions about the beliefs and dispositions of the heir to his country's throne, of Ken, and of Eve.

These considerations suggest that even an analysis of beliefs as "clusters" of dispositions will be inadequate. (Given a certain type of person (who has a given belief) with certain unusual wants, fears, etc., unusual dispositions usually obtain.) But the application to beliefs of the related notion of a *law* cluster concept will be viewed differently. See the discussion of theoretical entities, below, esp. note 27.

If, then, beliefs are not PPEs, not dispositions to act, and not a combination of these two, we still have to say what they are. Let us turn, then, to a consideration of another analysis of belief which has been presented in the literature.

William James, for example, has written of "that new psychic act . . . which I prefer to call 'belief'."[10] And C. A. Mace also talks of "the act of belief".[11] A similar, although more restricted, claim is made by Sándor Ferenczi in discussing the differences between (a) blind belief which has been accepted on some authority, and (b) belief based on adequate grounds. Calling the former "belief" and the latter "conviction", he claims that "belief is distinguished from conviction in that belief is an act of repression, conviction on the other hand, an impartial passing of judgment."[12] Since both acts of repression and the passing of judgments are acts, it follows that Ferenczi is required to claim also that at least certain species of beliefs are acts.

Are, then, beliefs acts? There are several philosophical characterizations of acts available. On none of these characterizations are beliefs (or the having of beliefs) acts. On one

---

[10]*The Principles of Psychology* (New York, Henry Holt & Co., 1923), vol. 2, Chap. 21, p. 287.

[11]"Beliefs," *Proceedings of the Aristotelian Society*, vol. 29 (1928-29), p. 250.

[12]"Belief, Disbelief, and Conviction," *Further Contributions to the Theory and Technique of Psycho-analysis* (London, The Hogarth Press, Ltd., and The Institute of Psycho-analysis, 1951), pp. 442f.

analysis, acts are those things which are done intentionally. But one does not intentionally believe some statements; nor, of course, does he believe it unintentionally, nor non-intentionally.

Others claim that acts are those things which one can be said to be doing (at some given time). But although one can be listening to an Eric Dolphy recording, or praying to Allah, he cannot be believing something. (Believing something isn't something that one does.)

If, moreover, we look (independently of philosophical presuppositions as to how the notion of acts is best analyzed) at those characteristics which acts usually have, beliefs, or the having of beliefs, have *none* of these. For example, performing acts can be tiring; acts can be done sloppily, or slowly, or carefully; they can take time to complete; they can be postponed. They can be done intentionally or non-intentionally. They can be made part of the plans for a given day's (year's) activities. But one cannot plan to believe at some future time that Allah is worship-worthy; one cannot believe something slowly, nor unintentionally, nor sloppily, nor carefully. Nor can one take several hours to believe something, which, of course, is not to say that one cannot take several hours to come to believe something. Nor can one tire by believing something, even by *believing* that he is working hard (even if his realization that he is working hard might bring him to stop work on the grounds of his being tired). There seem to be no grounds for the claim that beliefs, or having of beliefs, are acts. Note that what I say above holds of "mental" acts as well as of "physical" ones (assuming this distinction to be somewhat presystematically clear).

We have shown, then, that beliefs are not PPEs, nor dispositions or tendencies, nor PPEs combined with dispositions, nor acts. Before continuing with the presentation of our more positive statements about the notion of belief, it is important to see a major implication of the preceding arguments.

It has sometimes been argued that what is essential to something's being mental is its being in one's consciousness (at some time). Titchener, for example, equates the mind with consciousness.[13] He takes psychology to be the science of mind, but adds that this is an acceptable definition only "if 'mind' is understood to mean simply the sum total of mental processes experienced by the individual in his lifetime."[14]

If, however, we review what has already been said above, it can be seen that only PPEs will be experienced by an individual. In spite of this fact, we hold that certain things which are not PPEs are nonetheless mental entities. Included in these are tendencies (such as that of finding a certain person's humor rather droll) and other non-PPEs (such as beliefs).

The characterization of something mental as something experienced by an individual is, therefore, inadequate. We cannot, that is, accept the equation of the mind with consciousness.

Let us consider Freud's claim: "We become obliged then to take up the position that it is both untenable and presumptuous to claim that whatever goes on in the mind must be known to consciousness."[15] What this and the above argument do (among other things), is to cut against a certain model of the mind which is presupposed in much of our commonsense thoughts about the mind, even though this model is inadequate. The model is that of the mind as one's consciousness. (But it is of course not merely a common-sense model. One finds it proposed in systematic psychologies of the past, e.g., Hume, Titchener, etc.)

But this model is, minimally, grossly misleading. For there are many mental entities which are simply *not* the *kinds* of things which can be presented to consciousness. It can be seen, then, that an equating of the mind with consciousness is the result of confusion. And the confusion is that made by assuming that something is a mental entity if and only if it is a PPE, that is, by equating the mental with the phenomenological.

---

[13]*An Outline of Psychology* (New York, The Macmillan Co., 1896), p. 296.
[14]*Ibid.*, p. 9.
[15]"The Unconscious," trans. C. M. Baines, *Collected Papers* (London, The Hogarth Press and the Institute of Psycho-analysis, 1957), vol. 4, p. 99.

Differently stated, if we think of the mind as a system or organ of an individual (viz., an MP) with certain functions (e.g., that of remembering), capacities (e.g., that of analogizing), components (e.g., consciousness, memory, and perhaps also the preconscious (Freud's Pcs), etc.),[16] then we can see that there are many things in the mind which are, therefore, mental, but which *cannot* be present in consciousness.

The distinction, then, between consciousness and the mind is, I hope, clear by now. As SOME MAJOR errors in modern philosophy, I take it, arise out of a blurring of this distinction (e.g., the tendency to hold an individual to be the only one who can really know about his own mental life, to think of the mental as the private, the internal, etc.), it is important to keep this distinction clear. I will try to do this partly by not holding the phrase 'in the mind' to be an acceptable variant of 'in one's consciousness'.

To take just one example, Sartre seems to accept the position that something is mental only if it is, or can be, phenomenologic-ally presented.[17] This position is later used as one aspect of his criticism of certain Freudian notions of mental processes which are unobservable to the persons who possesses them,[18] in his *Being and Nothingness*,[19] esp. pp. 50-54. Freud himself argues against any theory which equates the mental with the pheno-

---

[16]Compare this with: "The psyche is the mind. In modern psychiatry the psyche is regarded in its own way as an 'organ' for the individual. . . . [T]he psyche . . . like other organs, possesses its own form and function, its embryology, gross and microscopic anatomy, physiology and pathology." (*Psychiatric Dictionary*, ed. L. E. Hinsie and R. J. Campbell (New York, Oxford University Press, 1960), *q.v.* 'psyche', p. 588).

[17]Consider in the *following* context his claim: "A pure consciousness . . . is all lightness, all translucence." (*The Transcendence of the Ego: An Existentialist Theory of Consciousness*, trans. F. Williams and R. Kirkpatrick (New York, The Noonday Press, Inc., 1966) p. 42).

[18]Proposed, e.g., by Freud in "The Unconscious," *op. cit.* Cf., e.g., C. Brenner, *An Elementary Textbook of Psychoanalysis* (Garden City, N.Y., Doubleday & Co., Inc., 1957), p. 14.

[19]*Being and Nothingness: An Essay on Phenomenological Ontology*, trans. H. E. Barnes (New York, Philosophical Library, 1956).

menological,[20] and would, therefore, presumably not hold the Sartrean criticism to be too weighty.

It may be noted in passing that recent psychology has almost no inclination to suppose that the individual is the only one who can really know about his mental life. It suggests, rather, that people are often very poor judges about such matters. Consider the following comment on determining attitudes by indirect means (i.e., by means other than by asking the individual what his attitudes are): "One of the principal advantages of such measurement . . . lies in the possibility of concealing from the individual the intent of the measurement; this again may make for better measurement."[21]

Having, then, distinguished the mental from the phenomenological, and having shown that beliefs are not phenomenological, nor dispositional, etc., we still have to address the question of what beliefs are. In order for us to do this, let us briefly consider a recent discussion of the rather similar notion of wanting. Brandt and Kim[22] suggest that in the notion of wants we see the embodiment in ordinary language of certain common-sense psychological statements (laws). As the speaker learns to speak (in this case: English) they claim, he therein accepts a certain theory of human behavior. It can be shown, furthermore, that someone understands what the word 'want' means by showing that he accepts the majority of a set of claims which relate wanting to behaving in certain ways, to thinking certain thoughts, etc.

To quote: "The word 'want' has the meaning it does for us because we believe roughly the statements listed below."[23] These "statements . . . can be viewed as a small-scale psychological

---

[20]E. g., "But we may reply that . . . [such a] theory . . . simply begs the question by asserting 'conscious' to be an identical term with 'mental', and that it is clearly at fault in denying psychology the right to account for its most common facts, such as memory, by its own means." ("A note on the Unconscious in Psycho-Analysis," Collected Papers, vol. 4, p. 22).

[21]D. Krech and R. S. Crutchfield, Theory and Problems of Social Psychology (New York, McGraw-Hill Book Co., Inc., 1948), p. 246.

[22]"Wants as Explanations of Actions," Journal of Philosophy, vol. 60 (1963), pp. 425-434.

theory which is implicity embedded in our everyday understanding of events or processes involving wanting, feelings of
joy and disappointment, and the like. The meaning of 'wanting'
is anchored in this theory."[24]

I think that this position is correct, but I think it important
to explain just what this "everyday understanding" amounts
to. As we learn our native language, we *also* learn various facts
about the world we live in. Included here are facts about
human behavior learned in virtue of our living in society for all
our lives. Man can learn much, that is, about (human) behavior
without going into the laboratory to run carefully controlled
experiments on gerbils. It is in virtue of such very general
facts that we are in a position to make certain very abstract
claims about human nature. (At this point the most daring
comments of the philosopher approach those of the most philosophical musings of the scientist. We might ask, for example,
whether the majority of the middle chapters of Chomsky's
Cartesian Linguistics is linguistics or philosophy of mind/
language, and I think it is clearly all of these. A similar point
can be made with any number of articles dealing with subjects
which border on philosophy and some science.[25])

To state this view another way, as language-possessing individuals of a society, we have in addition to the native speaker's
grasp of his language, certain assumptions about various phenomena. Among these is that of human behavior. In expressing
the most firmly accepted or central of these assumptions, the
deepest-embedded of these, we present philosophical reflections
on these phenomena (in this context: on human nature).

The Brandt-Kim paper, then, presents us with certain very
abstract claims about the relationship between wants and their
manifestations. We accept these insofar as they express some
of the most firmly accepted of our assumptions about behavior.
As suggested above, these will be reflected in our language.

---

[23]*Ibid.*, p. 426.
[24]*Ibid.*, pp. 427f.
[25]For example, M. Ginsberg, "Katz on Semantic Theory and 'Good',"
Journal of Philosophy, vol. 63 (1966), pp. 517-521.

What I want to say in applying this position to the analysis of beliefs is that the term 'belief' is a theoretical construct in a common-sense (non-systematized) theory. In this respect it is similar to the term 'want'. Below we shall show certain rather basic ways in which beliefs are different from wants, but I think it more central for the moment to sketch just what is involved in claiming that the terms 'want' and 'belief' are theoretical constructs. As this is done elsewhere in philosophical literature,[26] I will be brief.

Theoretical constructs are *terms* which appear in the hypotheses of some theory. They express concepts ("theoretical concepts"), such as those of mass and electron-bonding (in physics and physical chemistry, respectively), which are used in the statement of some theory, such as chemistry, socio-economics, etc.[27]

These theoretical constructs are such that those entities ("theoretical entities") which are referred to by them are not observable. For example, the terms 'mass', 'psi function', 'electromagnetic field', 'ego strength', and 'internalization of a transformational grammar' are theoretical constructs and, correspondingly, one cannot observe mass, psi functions, electromagnetic fields, etc. Contrast this with condensation in a Wilson cloud

---

[26]E.g., R. Carnap, "The Methodological Character of Theoretical Constructs," *Minnesota Studies in the Philosophy of Science*, vol. 1, ed. H. Feigl and M Scriven (Minneapolis, University of Minnesota Press, 1959), pp. 38-76; C. Hempel, *Fundamentals of Concept Formation in Empirical Science* (Chicago, The University of Chicago Press, 1962); A. Kaplan, *The Conduct of Inquiry: Methodology for Behavioral Science* (San Francisco, Chandler Publishing Co., 1964), pp. 55ff.

[27]As mentioned above, this analysis may be compared with one involving the notion of law cluster concepts. My analysis of belief can be roughly construed as holding that belief is a law cluster concept (as opposed to a cluster concept). Note that the position actually proposed below would then be seen as maintaining, *in addition*, certain epistemological assumptions about beliefs (viz., they are non-observables) where a law cluster analysis would be noncommittal.

For a fine presentation of the notions of cluster concepts and law cluster concepts, see H. Putnam, "The Analytic and the Synthetic," *Minnesota Studies in the Philosophy of Science*, vol. 3, ed. H. Feigl and G Maxwell (Minneapolis, University of Minnesota Press, 1966), pp. 358-397, esp. pp. 378f.

chamber, the complete lack of movement of a schizophrenic in a catatonic state, the phonetically identical pronunciation of 'e' in 'merrily', 'a' in 'Mary', and 'a' in 'married' by someone who speaks a certain dialect of American English, etc., all of which are observable.[28]

---

[28]I *would* like to be able to make explicit what constitutes being an observable other than by giving a few examples. The following will be helpful, although perhaps not adequate for all considerations.

We might begin by distinguishing between two types of phrase: (1) 'observe x', and, (2) 'observe that s', where 'observe' may be replaced by other verbs of perception, where the range of 's' is all declarative sentences, and where the range of 'x' is all noun phrases other than those resultant from nominalizing sentences. (We will consider several formulations of what is to count as nominalizing sentences below.)

These two types of phrase can be used in reporting different types of observation, which we might call non-sentential observation and sentential observation, respectively. Examples of the first type are seeing the tree, tasting the cheese, observing the tom-cat, seeing the turned-on light bulb, hearing the man, hearing the sound of some bell, and observing the texture of a piece of cloth. Examples of the second type are observing that the tree is alive, seeing that the tabby tom-cat is chasing another cat, observing that the switched-on lightbulb is too bright to look at, and tasting that sugar has been added to the tea.

One convenient delineation of the nominalizing of a declarative sentence (in English) would be to take it to be preceding that sentence by 'that' (and, if necessary, altering the intonation pattern of the sentence slightly in order to maintain naturalness of expression). We could then specify that the notion of observation relevant to the text is non-sentential observation.

One problem with this is that given this limited notion of the nominalization of sentences, some non-sentential observation phrases seem to be equivalent to certain sentential observation phrases. Thus, 'observing x as y' (in which 'x as y' would not count as an example of a nominalized sentence) seems to be equivalent to 'observing that z is y', where 'x' and 'y' range over (and 'z' is replaceable by *some*) noun phrases other than nominalized sentences (in the first delineation of this notion), and where observing that z is y does *not* entail, imply, or suggest that z is in fact y.

For example, someone sees a Mayan religious sceptre as a royal sceptre (which, ex hypothesi, it is not). This amounts to his seeing that a given object is a royal sceptre (in a sense of seeing—perhaps introduced in this work—in which this does not entail, imply, or suggest that the object in question is in fact a royal sceptre).

If this is so, then we might consider 'x as y' as a second kind of nominalization, here, of the sentence 'z is y' in which 'z' is deleted and 'x' is introduced, etc. If we accept a broader (but not so well-defined) notion of the nominalization of sentences, of which the "that" nominaliza-

Furthermore, and rather importantly for explicating the status of beliefs, each theoretical construct appears in the hypotheses of the theory along with certain other constructs. Thus, theoretical constructs are explicated by interrelating them with other theoretical constructs. As these theoretical constructs are introduced, *en masse,* they are also interrelated with the data they are intended to explain and make intelligible. First, then, (to present a reconstruction of a theory) we interrelate various of

---

tion and the "as" nominalization are two instances, we may then say that the sense of observation relevant is still that of non-sentential observation (in what amounts to a second sense of this notion).

In passing, I might mention at this point that a candidate for a third type of nominalization of sentences is one resulting in 'x to be y' (e.g., in "perceiving x to be y"). Consider here a comment made by Goodman in his discussion of art as representation: "A picture never merely represents x, but rather represents x *as* a man or represents x *to be* a mountain, or represents *the fact that x is* a melon." *Languages of Art* (New York, The Bobbs-Merrill Co., Inc., 1968), p. 9 (his emphases).)

Alternatively, we might retain the first, narrower notion of the nominalization of sentences and say that the observation relevant to the discussion in the text are those instances of non-sentential observation not reportable using non-sentential observation phrases equivalent to any sentential observation phrases. (I prefer the former formulation employing the broader notion of nominalization.)

We might now say that something is an observable, relative to the theory in question, if and only if it is in the extension of some term 'x' such that something would count an observing x (in the relevant sense of observation). (We might in this context consider Goodman's comments about the relativity of manifest and dispositional predicates in *Fact, Fiction, and Forecast* (second edition, New York, The Bobbs-Merrill Co., Inc., 1965), p. 41, note 7.)

Thus, for example, since nothing would count as observing an electromagnetic field, electromagnetic fields are *not* observables, even though something *would* count as observing *that* an electromagnetic field is for example, (partly) responsible for the particular arrangement of certain iron filings in a certain region of space. (The former, but not the latter, is the relevant type of observation.)

Similarly, certain formulations of a casual theory of perception might hold that one cannot ("really") observe or perceive physical objects, e.g., chairs, although one *can* observe, for example, *that* a chair is heavy. In such a formulation (theory), physical objects are not observables. (Certain critics of a casual theory of perception might then be understood as arguing, inter alia, that physical objects be granted the status of observables, rather than that, say, of theoretical constructs, in one's epistemology.)

these constructs in general hypotheses, or, in some cases, by definitions. This amounts to our having a set of sentences in which the terms in question (the theoretical constructs of the theory) appear. These sentences provide us with a statement of the characteristics of the theory's theoretical entities, of how these entities interact with one another, etc. The several constructs and hypotheses are then related to observables by the interpretations incorporated in the theory. What this amounts to is the presence of examples which illustrate the concepts and hypotheses of the theory (e.g., the infant's sucking its thumb illustrating the notion of oral gratification).

To use the Hempelian model, a theory is a net. At each knot (or what we might also call node) is some theoretical construct. Let us here talk of nodal constructs and similarly of such a theoretical entity as a nodal entity. The several nodes are connected by strings which represent hypotheses and definitions. Finally, and exterior to the uninterpreted theory (net) itself are various anchoring strings. These are interpretations of the theory which amount to relating the theory with what is observable, what is to be explained by the theory.[29]

If we apply this notion of theoretical constructs to the question at hand, we can interpret the words 'want' and 'belief' as theoretical constructs which are at two of the nodes in the net of the psychological theory in which they appear. The strings uniting them are hypotheses about the behavior of MPs and definitions of some of the theoretical constructs in terms of others.

Accepting, then, that beliefs are nodal entities of a psychological theory, we can now explain why we will not attempt to give a simple definition of the term 'belief'. The word means what it does because of the theoretical hypotheses in which it appears and because of the facts that the theory holds to be explained given the presence of given beliefs. Since the term means what it does because of the many theoretical inter-

---

[29]See C. Hempel, *Fundamentals of Concept Formation in Empirical Science, op. cit.,* p. 36, for the original formulation of the net metaphor.

connections between it and other constructs,[30] we will not show what the term 'belief' means by giving a simple analysis, but rather by making explicit (some of) those statements involving the notion of belief which are held to be most central to the (common-sense) theory. It follows from this analysis that there will be no sharp line of demarcation between those statements held to define what beliefs are and those which are derived from empirical investigation. The statements I will suggest as delineating our notion of belief are, I think, among the most central of our presuppositions about beliefs. It is to this that we should now turn.

It can be seen that although wants and beliefs are both mental nodal entities (i.e., entities referred to by theoretical constructs which have the status of being at knots or nodes in the Hempelian net metaphor, and which appear in a psychological theory), they are not identical to one another. To see this, let us consider just *some* of the central statements proposed in the Brandt-Kim paper:

(c) If daydreaming about p is pleasant to s, then x *wants* p.

(d) If x *wants* p, then, under favorable conditions, if x judges that doing A will probably lead to p and that not doing A will probably lead to not-p, x will feel some impulse to do A.

(f) If x *wants* p, then, under favorable conditions, if p occurs, without the simultaneous occurrence of events x doesn't want, x will be pleased.[31]

We can see that substituting the word 'believes' for 'wants' in these sentences, we will no longer find them acceptable. And this shows that beliefs and wants are clearly distinguishable.

---

[30]If we view Tolman's belief-value matrix ("A Psychological Model," *Toward a General Theory of Action*, ed. T. Parsons and E. A. Shils (New York, Harper & Row, Inc., 1965), pp. 279-361) as discussing beliefs, wants, and consciousness (rather than what Tolman takes to be the technical, behavioristically-defined notions of "beliefs", etc., we can see a psychologist's sketch of such a theory.

[31]*Op. cit.*, p. 427, emphases mine.

We can now propose several statements which will serve as examples of the central statements of our common-sense psychological theory which delineate what beliefs are. The following will be labeled "Ta", etc., to show their status as statements of our theory. They may be compared with statements (a)-(f) in the Brandt-Kim paper.

(Ta) If, given that (at time t_0) x did not want y, but now (at time t_1) suddenly develops a strong desire for y, and thereby becomes happy, then he believes that it is possible that he obtain or that he has obtained y.

(Tb) If, given that (at time t_0) x wanted y, but now (at time t_1) suddenly develops a strong aversion to y, finding it extremely unattractive, and thereby feels depressed, then he believes that it is extremely likely that he obtain or that he has obtained y.

(Tc) If x wishes that not-p were the case, then x believes that p is the case.

(Td) If x believes that doing A will probably lead to y and that not doing A will probably lead to not-y, then, under favorable conditions, if x wants y, x will have some tendency to do A.

(Te) If x believes that obtaining some M is a way of bringing y about, then, under favorable conditions, if x wants y, x will be more likely to notice an M that he would otherwise have been.

(Tf) If x believes that y alone occurs, then, under favorable conditions, if x wants y, x will be more pleased than if y alone hadn't occurred.

Note that the phrase 'under favorable conditions' is added to avoid situations in which the individual is physically exhausted, under the influence of certain drugs, etc., etc. The 'alone' in Tf is to avoid complications in which y is accompanied by several simultaneously occurring events which x doesn't want.

These six have been presented in order to bring out (partially) the difference between our notions of believing and wanting. We can propose still more defining statements in this work, but in order to do so, we are in need of an extremely important distinction.

The distinction is that between belief and judgment. This distinction has sometimes been blurred in the literature,[32] but this is unfortunate yet fortunately avoidable.

A judgment is the same as a realization, with the following exception. It is strongly suggested by the claim that someone realized that p, that p is true. But the claim that one judged that p has no such implication. (Note that in the discussion in note 28, above, we were similarly faced with a need to introduce a notion which was *non*-truth-evaluational (did *not* evaluate in terms of truth value) when we talked of observing that p *not* entailing, implying, or suggesting that p (was in fact true). That slight warping of ordinary English was brought about by a lacuna in the language.) I take it, then, that 'judgment' is a generic term which can refer to one's coming to a realization, seeing or deciding that something is the case, etc. Judging is, then, a mental act (unlike a belief or the having of a belief).

We assume that one's judging something to be so is a manifestation of certain of his beliefs. We can formulate this as the following:

(Tg) If x believes that p, then, under favorable conditions, and unless there are some factors which prevent that belief from being manifested in the judgment that p, x will, upon considering whether or not p, judge that p (is the case).

The second clause ("and unless . . . in the judgment that p") allows for the influence of fatigue, drugs, etc., as well as for the possibility of unconscious beliefs.

Rather than continuing with the enterprise of proposing

---

[32]E. G., G. F. Stout, "judgments is the Yes-No consciousness . . . I use the term Belief as a convenient variant for Judgment." (*Analytic Psychology* (London, Swan Sonnenschein & Co., Ltd., 1896), p 97) and, William James, who talks of "that new psychic act which Brentano calls 'judgment', but which I prefer to call 'belief.'" (*op. cit.*, vol. 2, p. 287)

more theoretical statements which define beliefs, let us consider for a moment the kinds of theoretical statements which can be proposed. We have, of course, statements (hypotheses) about when beliefs will be manifest in behavior. More precisely, we will have hypotheses which state which set of wants, beliefs, etc. will be manifested in certain behavior at certain times. In addition, some of our hypotheses deal with the conditions under which beliefs (and wants) are generated or destroyed. If, for example, we know that Tracy is awakened in the early morning by Mushrooms (her playful kitten) who is tickling her, that Tracy then stares directly in Mushrooms' direction, giggles as Mushrooms rubs its whiskers across her nose, and say 'Oh, Mushrooms!' (*not* trying to get the cat's attention, etc.,) we have excellent reason to suppose that Tracy now believes that there is a kitten in her vicinity. But it needn't be the case that there is *any* want that we want to claim has just been generated in Tracy, i.e., which Tracy has just come to have.

What this suggests is that since we are interested in more of a delineation of the concept of belief, we might now turn in more detail to the problem of the generation of beliefs. In the next chapter we *will* address ourselves to this problem, in the context of answering the question of how to model the phenomenon of what I will call the "self-ascription of beliefs".

Chapter II

THE SELF-ASCRIPTION OF BELIEFS

In the preceding chapter we tried to explain, sketchily, what beliefs are, and secondarily, why certain earlier philosophical analyses of the notion of belief were inadequate ones.

It is now time to turn to another set of problems concerning this concept. These problems arise out of the fact that individuals at times claim that they have certain beliefs. The attribution to oneself of a belief, which we shall refer to below as the self-attribution or the self-ascription of a belief, has several interesting characteristics.

First, one can answer an indefinitely large number of questions about whether he has a given belief or not with no hesitation at all. Consider, for example, how quickly you can answer *whether you believe* that one is a smaller number than five, that Julius Caesar is dead, that you're in Ann Arbor, that you speak English, that Swedish is an Indo-European language, that da Vinci was a great artist and thinker, that you have light blue eyes, that your left hand is clenched, that Nietzsche is a wise man, etc. Not only can one answer these and other questions, can make or refrain from making self-attributions of beliefs, but in an indefinitely great number of cases of earnest self-ascriptions of beliefs, we take it that the person making these self-ascriptions is correct. Exceptions to this, esp. cases in which one makes a self-ascription of a belief, is not attempting to deceive others, yet in which we think nonetheless that the person does *not* have this belief are often if not always cases of self-deception. Consider as an example of this the individual who earnestly claims that he believes that all people are equal and yet who is actually prejudiced against, say, Orientals. We will return to and question this example below.

Secondly, in some situations the appropriate answer to a

self-attribution of a belief ('I think that you should talk to your faculty adviser if you want good advice on that matter.') is *not* addressed to whether or not the belief is in fact held by that individual ('Oh, you don't think that at all.'), but rather to whether the belief itself is true or not ('The faculty adviser is the *worst* person to talk to about that.')

We will presently address ourselves to these two phenomena. In this chapter, I will attempt to show how it is that an individual can so readily and accurately assert that he has or hasn't a certain belief. I shall postpone an explanation of the second phenomenon described above until the next chapter.

Although we have already rejected Hume's analysis of belief, it is interesting to note that it does allow for answers to some of our present questions. As an answer to the question of what a belief is, Hume says that it is a characteristic PPE present in consciousness (at some time) concurrently with a certain thought (that which is believed),[1] or, alternatively, that it is a thought present in consciousness (at some given time) with a certain minimal degree of clarity and detail.[2] Given this, we can see how to answer the first main question of this chapter, viz., how does one have the capacity of making or refraining from making self-attributions of beliefs with the accuracy one in general does? Given a Humean analysis of beliefs, we could say that one has this capacity because of one's general capacity to describe those things which are in one's phenomenal field; to describe, that is, what we have called PPEs. It is also suggestive of an explanation of why one is so rarely wrong about whether he has a given belief or not. For it is rarely the case, it might be argued, that one mis-describes one of his present PPEs.

But since the answers are based on an analysis which is

---

[1] "An opinion, therefore, or belief may be most accurately defin'd, A LIVELY IDEA RELATED TO OR ASSOCIATED WITH A PRESENT IMPRESSION." (*Treatise*, Book I, Part III, Sect. VII, p. 96, his capitalization) Cf. his *Inquiry*, Sect. 5, part 2.

[2] "Belief . . . is nothing but *a more vivid and intense conception of any idea.*" (*Treatise*, Book I, Part III, Sect. X, pp. 119f., italics his.) Cf. his *Inquiry*, Sect. 5, part 2.

quite inadequate on other grounds, we cannot avail ourselves of the answers which it provides to our present questions.

In order to put ourselves in a position to answer these questions and thereby to understand the concept of belief better, let us first examine a somewhat uncomplicated case. This will perhaps suggest a theoretical framework into which these phenomena can be placed. After that we will examine more difficult cases and see to what extent our provisory framework is in need of revision.

Case 1: We go with our friend Paul to a museum. In one of the galleries, we see Paul looking directly at a portrait of someone's uncle which is dominated by a huge white beard. We see Paul start to stroke his clean-shaven chin, and we see him pointing to the portrait while complaining that in *these* days fullbearded men are often looked at as a bit eccentric.

Let us refer to the belief that the man in the portrait has a beard as belief B1. Now at this point we are willing to assert that Paul holds belief B1, i.e., thinks that the man in the portrait has a beard (as indeed he has). What are our grounds for this?

In order to answer the above question of how we can justify our claim that Paul holds belief B1, I will present a general discussion of the problem of providing grounds for any belief-ascription. In this context we can then return to the specific belief-ascription of case 1. After all of this, I will consider a different belief-ascription (in a case yet to be presented) in order to introduce the final statement of our answer to the question of how an individual can so readily and accurately assert that he has or hasn't a given belief.

We can divide the reasons which we could call upon to substantiate belief-ascription into two groups. The first of these is associated with the way in which beliefs are generated, i.e., in which an individual comes to have certain beliefs. The second is associated with the ways in which beliefs are partially effective in bringing about certain behavior, states, etc., of an individual who has the beliefs in question.

Before addressing case 1 directly, then, let us for a moment consider the first of these two sets of reasons. What grounds do we have on the basis of which we might delineate which beliefs a given individual can or cannot have? We assume, for example, that as a result of looking at something, the observer can come to have certain beliefs about what he is looking at. Furthermore, some beliefs one can come to are rather sophisticated beliefs, such as those beliefs which are complex to such a degree that we assume that they can be held only by an individual with a language. (We will refer to this claim below after the examples of the next paragraph.)

Among these are, for example, the beliefs that (a) a given individual is the spouse of the oldest sibling of one's maternal grandfather, that (b) Guernica is considered by many to be a disastrous example of how a highly organized military can efficaciously destroy a defenseless civilian population, and, that (c) the amount of energy which theoretically can be released from a given substance of mass m is equal to m times a constant, viz., the square of the speed of light through a vacuum, i.e., the claim which interprets the equation $E=mc^2$.

What the above claim amounts to is that there are some beliefs, such as (a)-(c), above, such that if we assume that a given individual speaks no language at all, then there is *no* (non-verbal) evidence which would justify us in attributing them to him. On the other hand, these same beliefs are such that there is some non-verbal evidence which would justify us in ascribing them to a given individual who does speak some language.[3]

For example, suppose someone (who speaks, say, English) and a dog (which speaks, of course, no language) are sitting

---

[3]Hampshire makes the more sweeping claim that dogs, as an example of living things which have no language, cannot have *any* beliefs, indeed that it is unintelligible to attribute beliefs to dogs since they cannot make verbal announcements of their beliefs. (*Thought and Action* (London, Chatto and Windus, 1959), p. 141.) I reject this stronger claim (and thereby agree with Wittgenstein, *Philosophical Investigations*, (trans. G. E. M. Anscombe (Oxford, Basil Blackwell, 1963), Part II, Sect. i, p. 174)).

in a room, and we say loudly and clearly in their presence that *if* Guernica is considered by many to be a disastrous example of how a highly organized military can efficaciously destroy a defenseless civilian population, *then* he should raise his hand (or paw). Suppose furthermore that the person raises his hand and the dog raises a paw. We count what the person has done as evidence for his believing that Guernica is considered by many to be a disastrous example of how a highly organized military can efficaciously destroy a defenseless civilian population. But we do not count what the dog has done as such evidence. And the reason for this is that we assume that the person understood our request, did believe Guernica to be &c., thought that he would follow our instructions by raising his hand, and consequently raised it. But in the case of the dog, we either do not suppose what we have said is in any way relevant to his lifting his paw (perhaps he was merely parroting the person's movement), or assume that it was his taking our statement as a command for him to lift his paw, but do *not* assume that it was his understanding what we said that brought it about that he raised his paw.

We assume a difference here not because of a difference between their behavior, but because of a difference in the two themselves.[4] We will go into this in much more detail in our last chapters when discussing the question of whether robots have beliefs and related questions.

In the above-mentioned case, we know ex hypothesi that Paul speaks English. Given that Paul does speak some language as a native speaker, we have excellent reason to suppose that he knows what a beard is, what color the color white is, what a man is, what a portrait painting is, etc. That is, that he can distinguish beards, the color white, men, portrait paintings, etc. from other things.

This is *not* to say that one could not distinguish such things from other things if one did not speak any language, but only

---

[4] See Ziff's "The Feelings of Robots," *Analysis,* vol. 19 (1959), esp. Sect. 7, where Ziff argues a similar point in another context.

that one's ability to speak a (natural) language such as English is excellent evidence for the supposition that he is capable of making these distinctions, that he knows what these things are, or, differently stated, that he understands or possesses these concepts.

Of course in cases where the individual being considered speaks no language (e.g., a dog or a cat), all of our evidence for the supposition that the individual has a given concept, e.g., that a cat can distinguish places where it may eat from those where it may not (the concept of an allowable eating place), must all be non-verbal. This is true for humans who speak no language (infants, the wolf-boy of India, etc.) as well as for dogs, cats, monkeys, etc. But as there *is* much non-verbal evidence, this is *not* an overwhelming problem.[5]

If we return to case 1 and consider it in the context of what has just been said, we can see that in case 1 there *is* secondary verbal evidence for the supposition that Paul has the concepts of a beard, a portrait, etc. (knows what a beard is, etc.) e.g., all of our conversations with Paul.

The importance of this is that we can now assume that it is possible for him to realize that what he sees is a portrait of a bearded man, i.e., is an instantiation of this kind of thing. That is, we now assume that he has the mental apparatus necessary to make this judgment. He can, we suppose, see what he sees as (an example of) such a portrait.

There are two things which we should notice about this. First, this assumes that seeing something as something (that is, seeing x as y, where the dummy variables 'x' and 'y' are typically

---

[5]In the case of the cat just mentioned, e.g., its running away when yelled at for eating from the dining room table (also evidence for its knowing it has done something wrong) but merely standing (bewildered?) when yelled at for eating from its own plate on the floor in its usual place is non-verbal evidence for the above-mentioned claim that the cat has the concept of an allowable eating place. I see no reason to accept Geach's claim that "brutes" (I assume that dogs qualify as brutes since Geach himself mentions them along with rats.) can have no concepts, or that there is no reason to ascribe concepts to brutes. (*Mental Acts: Their Content and Their Objects* (London, Routledge & Kegan Paul, 1964) p. v, and esp. pp. 16f.)

replaced by *different* noun phrases) is a case of classification, making a judgment, of classifying something as being a certain kind of thing, etc., and not, as it might at first seem, a case of perception.[6] If this is correct, then any philosophical or psychological analysis of the phenomenon of seeing x as y which employs as its model that of perception, rather than that of judgment, is doomed to failure.

Second, linguistic evidence (which is our grounds for supposing that an individual speaks some language) provides us with rather straightforward evidence for the claim that the individual has certain concepts, or, more precisely, certain concepts which are embodied in his native language. Of course, having a given concept amounts to being capable of determining whether something is an instantiation of that concept, i.e., being able to differentiate with respect to that concept. Differently stated, having the concept of being (an) x, of x-ness, amounts to being able to determine whether given instances are x. For example, having the concept of being a book (or, alternatively, of redness), amounts to being able to determine whether given instances (given colors) are books (are red).

As we have just said, linguistic evidence of the sort mentioned is support for the claim that the individual in question has certain concepts. But it is not the only kind of evidence for such a claim.

Let us consider, for example, the experiment in which rats are given an electric shock if they jump from a stage or platform at a card with a circle drawn on it, but are given food if they jump at a card with a triangle drawn on it. After many jumps, the rats jump consistently toward the triangle card, regardless of what is drawn on the other card, as long as the structure of the other figure does not approach that of a triangle. In so behaving, the rats are supplying us with evidence in support of the claim that they can differentiate between triangles and

---

[6]See note 28 of chapter I, where seeing x as y is considered to be a type of what I called sentential observation.

other figures. But this amounts to support for the claim that they have the concept of triangularity.[7]

Some psychologists do not find this a reasonable claim. Osgood, for example, in reviewing such experiments, asks skeptically, "should we conclude that the rat can understand the *abstract* concept of triangularity?"[8] Osgood seems to find it unreasonable to claim that mere rats could have abstract concepts. If he is presupposing a contrast between abstract and non-abstract concepts, perhaps he will be willing to accept the possession of less "abstract" concepts by rats. (I suppose that the concept of food might count here as a non-abstract concept.) If this is so, that is, if Osgood would be willing to claim that rats can have the concept of food, then his only argument is about a single application of the principle that non-verbal evidence can support the claim that a given individual has some concept and not with the general methodological acceptability of this principle.

If, rather, the term 'abstract' is somewhat redundant here, i.e., if Osgood thinks of *all* concepts as abstract, then perhaps he is being misled by the wording of the claim. Since all that having an (abstract) concept of C-ness amounts to is being able to tell whether a given something is an example of C-ness, this latter formulation of the claim might be more acceptable to him. (I will continue, however, to use the two wordings interchangeably, usually preferring the former because of its succinctness.)

If, however, Osgood would refuse to acknowledge such facts as evidence for the correct attribution of a concept, then he must provide grounds in support of his refusal to explain an empirical finding by what seems to be a reasonable hypothesis. In doing so, he would be required, as an experimental psychologist, to explain many rather varied aspects of experiments

---

[7]This experiment is reported in P. E. Fields, "Studies in concept formation. I: The development of the concept of triangularity by the white rat," *Comparative Psychology Monographs*, vol. 9 (1932). See e.g., p. 50.

[8]*Method and Theory in Experimental Psychology* (New York, Oxford University Press, 1956), p. 667, his emphasis.

all of which can be explained by assuming the possibility of concept-possession by animals. To see the variety, consider the following: (1) Rats learn where food is placed: "In experiment I the habitual response was modified by merely showing the rats the food in a new position. Knowledge of the new position of the food made the rats seek this new place rather than go to the table where they had been in the habit of finding food."[9] (2) A gorilla recognizes the experimenter and the experiments: "Visual memory of the experimenter after absence of ten months was observed, as was also memory of various features of the experimental situation and of several types of problem ten to eleven months after previous experience."[10] (3) Monkeys distinguish triangles from other shapes: "The monkeys learned to pick the more triangular of two objects, regardless of size, brightness, figure-ground relations, or rotation of the stimuli; change in the form of the correct training stimuli; or change from complete to incomplete or outlined stimuli."[11] (4) Octopuses discriminate between open and closed shapes: "This experiment establishes for the first time that octopuses can learn to discriminate accurately between stationary shapes" which are open and those which are closed.[12] (5) Porcupines fight with quills in different positions depending on whether or not they are fighting other porcupines: "Porcupines ward off all enemies, except those of their own species with erected quills. . . . In all minor quarrels they meet their own kind from the front and with adpressed quills, showing to that extent a consciousness of kind."[13] (6) Raccoons react differently to different intensities of

---

[9] N. R. F. Maier, "Reasoning in White Rats," *Comparative Psychology Monographs*, vol. 6 (1929), p. 81.

[10] R. M. Yerkes, "The Mind of a Gorilla. Part III. Memory," *Comparative Psychology Monographs*, vol. 5 (1928-29), p. 75.

[11] G. Andrew and H. F. Harlow, "Performance of Macaque Monkeys on a Test of the Concept of Generalized Triangularity," *Comparative Psychology Monographs,* vol. 19 (1948), p. 19.

[12] N. S. Sutherland, "The Shape-discrimination of Stationary Shapes by Octopuses," *The American Journal of Psychology*, vol. 76 (1963), p. 186.

[13] L. W. Sackett, "The Canada Porcupine: A Study of the Learning Process," *Behavior Monographs*, vol. 2 (1913), p. 79.

light: The raccoon "had been responding to the brightness and not to the pattern aspect of the stimulating conditions."[14] and (7) Cats learn to discriminate between various shapes, figure-ground contrasts, etc.: "The conclusion may also be drawn from the summarized data . . . that certain visual contours appear to be one of the variables in a total stimulus situation upon which their responses to the situation are dependent, and also . . . that these responses may be observed when similar objective stimulus patterns are presented under different conditions of size, brightness, position, etc."[15] Many more articles are, of course, readily available in the literature.

If we assume that animals like the cat, rat, etc., do have minds, then there is much evidence in support of the claims that they have (or can have) various concepts. The only ground left on which to substantiate the Osgood claim is the supposition that no non-human animal has a mind. There is excellent reason to reject such a claim (in articles such as the above). The more theoretical aspect of this issue (when to hold a given entity to be an MP) will be discussed in more detail in the last chapters.

Such evidence as just referred to, then, helps substantiate the claim that the individual, i, has some concepts. This of course allows us to conclude only that i is *capable* of taking something as exemplifying one of these concepts, and not that i does so in a given situation.

Knowing that Paul (in case 1) has the concept of a portrait, we can conclude that it is possible for Paul to see what he is staring at as a portrait. It does not follow, of course, that he does so; he needn't realize that what he sees is a portrait even though he has this concept.

Since this is the case, we have *not* established that Paul realizes that he is looking at a portrait of a bearded man, or even at a portrait (simpliciter).

[14]N. L. Munn, "Pattern and Brightness Discrimination in Raccoons," *Journal of Genetic Psychology*, vol. 37 (1930), p. 31.
[15]K. U. Smith, "Visual Discrimination in the Cat: A further study of the capacity of the cat for visual figure discrimination," *Journal of Genetic Psychology*, vol. 45, No. 2 (1934), p. 352.

On the other hand, we have a somewhat detailed notion of what factors might lead to his coming to this realization, and what might lead to his not doing so. If we know that he is attentively looking for portraits, for example, it is more likely that he will notice this museum work. If, however, we know that he is preoccupied with worries, e.g., about important financial matters, it is more likely that he will not take notice of something in his perceptual field.[16]

We have, that is, an ordering of PPEs with respect to the likelihood of one's noticing them, given that they are in one's perceptual field. We take it that it is more likely that one will notice a fairly large figure than an extremely small one, one which contrasts with its ground than one which blends with it, one group of PPEs involving complex interrelations between its member PPEs which one has learned to identify more than one which one hasn't,[17] etc.

Secondly, certain factors will change the probability of one's noticing something in one's perceptual field. Being emotionally upset, excited, terribly distraught, physically exhausted,[18] under certain drugs, etc., for example, make it more likely that one will *not* notice a PPE.

Both of these two kinds of assumption, viz., about which PPEs one is more likely to notice, and about what factors

---

[16]Cf. E. R. Hilgard, L. V. Jones, and S. J. Kaplan, "Conditioned Discrimination as related to Anxiety," *Journal of Experimental Psychology*, vol. 42, No. 2 (1951), esp. p. 98.

[17]Thus aesthetic appreciation involving recognizing themes, variations, balances (visual, auditory, etc.) is in part a matter of such ability, and partly responsible, it seems, for the common claim that aesthetic is subjective. Some simply cannot (unless they acquire certain abilities) categorize an object of aesthetic appreciation as is necessary for an adequate analysis and evaluation of that object.
Consider at this point the comment made recently by N. Goodman, "Pictures in perspective, like any others, have to be read; and the ability to read has to be acquired." (*Languages of Art, op. cit.*, p. 14).

[18]Cf. E. Fischbein, E. Pampu, and Al. Badoi, "L'utilisation des certaines activités de mémorisation dans le cadre de l'épreuve mixte pour la détermination de la fatigue," *Revue roumaine des sciences sociales*: Série de psychologie, vol. 8, No. 1 (1964), esp. pp. 31 and 34 where fatigue is shown to inhibit learning.

will result in one's overlooking PPEs do *not* involve what Hempel calls metrical ordering.[19] That is, these orderings allow us to determine which kind of PPE will be more likely to be noticed, or alternatively, which psychological, physical, pharmacological, etc., state of the individual will be more likely to distract one from noticing PPEs. On the other hand, not being a metrical ordering (in Hempel's sense), we *cannot* thereby determine if a PPE of one kind is twice or three times as likely to be noticed than one of another kind (or: psychological, etc., state of the individual will make it twice, etc. as likely that a given PPE will be noticed). That is, this ordering is ordinal rather than cardinal.

What is important here is to realize what factors will influence whether or not one takes a PPE to be of a certain kind. We have, to begin with, certain methods by which to determine whether a given individual has a given concept. If we determine that he does, we can conclude that it is possible for him to see a PPE as exemplifying that concept. Then we can cite factors which influence whether or not he will in fact see this PPE in that way, e.g., those influencing whether he will notice it at all (such as whether it (the figure) contrasts well with the ground), and those influencing *how* he will see it (such as his looking for the name 'Nina' camouphlaged in a sketch influencing him to identify a crop of hair in the sketch as the name 'Nina' written so as to look like a crop of hair).

Where there is an important difference between our ability to explain phenomena using the explanatory frameworks of the physical sciences and that using our common-sense psychological framework is in the neatness and assumed completeness of the knowledge of various relevant determining factors, i.e., of the independent variables involved. What is needed in psychological theory construction, *if* it is to attempt to base itself on the non-laboratory-generated theory being sketched in this work, yet be stronger in its predictive capacity than this one is, is the formulation of interrelations which allows for

---

[19]*Fundamentals of Concept Formation*, part 11 (esp. p. 61).

the neatness, completeness, preciseness, etc., attained in the physical sciences.[20]

Now in the case of Paul (case 1), the facts that he has the concepts of being a bearded man, a portrait, etc., that he is not psychologically upset, nor under drugs, nor mentally exhausted from having been performing the activity of examining paintings for a long period of time, etc., all give reason to suppose that Paul takes what is in front of him as a portrait of a bearded old man, as it in fact is.

This, however, is not all of the evidence available to us. As I said above, we have two kinds of evidence to call upon. The first is the evidence supporting the claim that a given belief has been *generated*. Roughly, this evidence consists of those factors which bring it about that the individual has the belief or beliefs in question. This has just been discussed. It can be noted in passing that we reject the claims of anachronistic belief-possession (e.g., the Rembrandt-Warhol case of chapter I) on the grounds that there is no way in which the given beliefs could possibly have been generated at the time in question. (Here: Rembrandt couldn't have known about Warhol.)

The second is the evidence which we explain by the supposition that a belief is held by the individual in question (not yet discussed here). Relevant here are some of the comments made in the first chapter in the context of sketchily delineating what beliefs are. Roughly, this evidence is what we take to be *manifestations* of some belief (and sometimes also manifestations of some want, etc.)

In the above case, I take it that Paul's stroking his beardless chin is evidence, but only rather weak evidence, for the claim that he holds belief B1. That he makes the comment that he does, however, is much stronger evidence for the attribution of this belief.

Why is all of this so? One of the relevant suppositions that

---

[20]Cf. Tolman, *op. cit.*, for the sketch of the basic framework for such a theory.

we are accepting is that Paul is at least somewhat interested in the paintings in the museum, or perhaps that he is concentrating intensely on them. (Which, if either, of these two we would assume in an actual situation would depend at least partly on what we know about Paul's general interest in (this kind of) art.)

Given this (and the obvious fact that his hands are free), it is not at all surprising that Paul then stroked his chin. It is somewhat likely that Paul would rub his chin in such a situation, and, importantly, only slightly more likely that he would do so given the added assumptions that he is examining the portrait and that he has belief B1. That is to say, we can explain Paul's stroking his chin rather easily without the assumption that he holds belief B1, by appeal to the facts that Paul is concentrating on art in a museum and that man such as Paul are prone to place their hand on their chin, rub their chin, etc. at such moments. (Whether this is typical only of (pretentious) men in our society since Rodin, or of all men is irrelevant so long as we know Paul to be a member of all such sets.) Since this is so, Paul's stroking his chin is only minor evidence for the claim that he has the belief in question.

In this context we can contrast Paul's chin-stroking with his making the comment he did while pointing to the portrait. The claim I wish to make and to argue for is that in the case imagined the ascription to Paul of belief B1 provides us with the most acceptable account of this behavior (the pointing and the commenting).[21]

In order to substantiate this claim, let us for a moment assume that Paul does *not* have this belief. What alternative explanations could we propose to account for the facts to be explained in this example? We have, first of all, to explain how it is that Paul can stand in front of a bearded man without being psychologically distraught, under the influence of any drugs, physically exhausted, etc., nonetheless speak English

---

[21]Consider in this context Gilbert H. Harman, "The Inference to the Best Explanation," *Philosophical Review,* vol. 74, No. 1 (Jan., 1965) pp. 88-95.

fluently and therefore have the concepts of a portrait, a beard, etc., and still not hold belief B1.

He might, e.g., have had his eyes closed during all of this time, due to eye strain. Or he might be blind. Or, if the painting is of a Scotsman in a kilt, painted with extremely fine facial features, and if Paul is rather ignorant of the dress of the Scots, he might have taken this to be a portrait of a bearded woman. Or Paul might be in a hypnotic trance with the instructions to stop at a given painting with a certain frame (so described to Paul that he thereby picks out the uncle's portrait) and, without at all noticing what the painting is of, to stop and stare "through" the painting.

Each of these assumptions is consistent with this example as it was originally stated. But in an actual situation we have very many facts which we call upon in the formulation of hypotheses about people's states (beliefs, wants), behavior, etc. and might have already eliminated all of these as viable hypotheses on the basis of such facts. We might, for example, have noticed that Paul's eyes were not closed, and thereby excluded the first of these hypotheses. And we might simply know that our old friend Paul is not at all blind, and thereby, knowing it to assume a false premise, not have considered the second, etc.

Of course these are merely the complications which arise when we attempt to explain how it is that under the circumstances imagined in the example this belief might not have been generated in Paul, i.e., how Paul might not have come to have this belief. We can leave this problem for the moment and turn to the even more difficult task of explaining his comment without appeal to the belief I finally want to ascribe to him.

How, then, might Paul point to the portrait in front of him, comment that in *these* days fullbearded men are often looked at as a bit eccentric, and yet *not* believe B1?

Let us try to explain this using the explanations just given in an attempt to explain how this belief might not be generated in such a situation. We may begin with the supposition that

Paul has not seen the painting at all because his eyes have been shut during the entire time that he has been facing it. We cannot of course say that he has just overheard someone mentioning that the painting is a portrait of a bearded man and that because of this Paul made his comment. This does provide us with an explanation of how he might point and comment as he does without having seen the portrait at all. It does not, however, do so without appeal to Paul's having belief B1. It does provide an explanation of his pointing and commenting, but with the following implicit steps. When Paul hears the comment that the painting is a portrait of a bearded man, he thereby comes to believe B1. That is, his hearing the comment generates the belief in question. As a consequence of this, plus perhaps a nostalgia for the days when man was under no inhibition to remain beardless, Paul made the comment he did.

Perhaps a more defensible alternative explanation *is* still available to us. We might suppose, for example, that just before Paul closed his eyes he noticed a man walk by who had an immense beard. Suppose further that Paul is not nostalgic for the days of the full beard, but is very content being clean shaven and indeed wishes everyone would be as neat as he is. Paul closes his eyes perhaps out of a slight (nauseous?) sensation in the pit of his stomach brought about by the sight of the immense beard. And, in an attempt to embarrass the bearded museum-goer into clean-shavenness, he points to where he takes the bearded man to be, and makes the comment he does.

What I have just provided is an alternative explanation of Paul's behavior. I take it that this is almost as good an explanation as one which would involve essential appeal to his having belief B1.

We could analyse some of the more subtle changes in assumption which this new explanation places on the case (e.g., divesting the pointing of its status as pointing at the portrait), but rather than that, let us concentrate instead on why the explanation involving this belief-ascription (of B1) is somewhat superior to this alternative explanation.

In Paul's comment there is a certain temporal contrast being made (the "in *these* days"). By assuming that Paul believes B1, that he takes this bearded man to be of another age and society in contrast with the cleanshavenness of his (Paul's) society, that he is a bit nostalgic for beards, etc., we explain why the contrast Paul makes is made. But in the alternative explanation, this contrast is left unexplained. (He might just as well have said, "I think bearded men are a bit eccentric!", if we employ this alternative explanans, but hardly so if we ascribe the belief B1 to him.)

I suppose, however, that in an actual situation we would have much stronger reasons for accepting one of these two competing explanations instead of the other, e.g., that we know that Paul like beards, or we know that he dislikes them strongly, that we see that Paul's eyes are shut, or are open, that we know that Paul is very polite, or likely to try to embarrass someone he does not take a liking to, etc.

On grounds such as these, then—those related to the generation and the manifestation of beliefs—we can justify *our* choosing to ascribe a belief to Paul, or to abstain from doing so.

Self-ascription of Beliefs

What are the implications of our above analysis (which suggested certain grounds for the ascription of beliefs to *others*) for the problem of self-ascription of beliefs? If we turn now to this problem, we are faced with the following dilemma:

What we are looking for is a model for the self-ascription of beliefs. If we take as our model that of how we ascribe beliefs to others, we are strongly tempted to say that (e.g., using case 1) *Paul* needn't notice that he (Paul) is in front of a portrait of a bearded man, that he (Paul) points to the portrait and comments as he does, in order to realize that he (Paul) holds belief B1. Without trying to define the notion of immediacy, we would at first like to say that his realization that he has this belief is much more immediate than that model seems to suggest. We will explain this immediacy, below.

Relevant to our search for an adequate model for the self-ascription of beliefs are the following considerations. We want to maintain the distinction between some individual's having a belief, and some individual's believing that he has that belief. (In order to see this distinction rather sharply, consider the difference between claiming that a cat believes that it is going to be hit, and claiming that the cat believes that it has the belief that it is going to be hit. The cat's quickly hiding under a chair is evidence for the first, but hardly for the second.)

In addition, we have rejected the position that a belief is a PPE. If, however, beliefs are not PPEs, they cannot be perceived by the individual. That is, having a belief is not a matter of perception. This much is, by now, obvious.

The tendency to model the self-ascription of beliefs on perception stems in part, but only in part, from the realization that in a great number of cases one needn't deliberate at all when asked before self-ascribing or refraining from self-ascribing a belief. This is just a fact which any adequate model of self-ascription of beliefs must illuminate.

One may be misled, however, by the kind of example which is first thought of. In this context we may consider the Empiricist influence on epistemology: in this century alone, e.g., for the logical positivists (e.g., Otto Neurath's "Protocol Sentences" trans. G. Schick, ed. A. J. Ayer, *Logical Positivism* (New York, The Free Press, 1966) and also for others (e.g., G. E. Moore's "Proof of an External World", *Proceedings of the British Academy*, vol 25 (1939), esp. pp. 144-145), the model for the assertion of a firm belief has been that of a belief about some perceptual phenomenon. (We needn't be interested here in arguments in the history of philosophy as to whether "ideas", or "notions", or "sense data", or "physical objects", or things of some other kind are what are phenomenally presented, perceived, etc.)

Instead of such a belief, which might keep us overly infatuated with the perception model, let us use for the present some other kind of belief, i.e., a belief which is not about any perceptual phenomenon.

In order to understand self-ascription of beliefs better, then, let us consider the belief which we shall refer to as belief B2.

> (B2) One's father was the final arbiter on all matters of
> importance to the family (in which one grew up).

A belief such as this has the advantage that it will allow us to avoid, if possible, any unwarranted tendencies to support a perception model for the self-ascription of beliefs.

Before we begin this discussion, we should distinguish the question we are asking from several other similar ones. As stated before, what we are trying to propose is a model which will provide us with an understanding of the phenomenon of self-attribution of beliefs. We want to answer the question of how it is that one so readily ascribes given beliefs to oneself with such a high degree of correctness.

I do not want to address myself to the question of what justifies one in claiming that he has a given belief, nor to the question of when one is being reasonable in claiming that he has a given belief (if indeed these amount to different questions). I am not interested here in what makes a given claim a reasonable one, nor in (which is slightly different) what makes one reasonable in making a given claim. The interest in reasonableness can lead us to an answer to the question in focus at the present time only if we assume that individuals hold only those beliefs that it is reasonable (rational, justifiable, etc.) for them to hold. (One needn't go into politics or religion to reject this assumption. Consider only a devoted mother who believes her son's claims of innocence of some deed which has been shown by overwhelmingly strong evidence to have been committed by the son.) Since this is so, the question of how to determine which of one's beliefs are justifiable is sufficiently different from the question we are interested in for us to ignore it here.

We will now consider another case. This will provide us with a problem sufficiently complex to suggest to us a more appropriate model for the self-attribution of beliefs. In addition, this will allow for an extended presentation of a case showing what we have called the generation of beliefs and the manifestation of beliefs. In the course of this presentation, we will also be laying the groundwork for the subsequent analysis of unconscious beliefs.

The case is the following: Several people are discussing their childhoods. The conversation has turned to the family power structure of the homes in which they grew up. One person comments that her family, as she remembers it, was run by her mother, and that her father turned most of his energies to the task of providing the mother and family with adequate (financial) support. Some comments are made at this point and then Tim says that he thinks [believes] that in *his* family, his *father* was the final arbiter on all matters of importance to the family.

This is the claim we will consider. Tim, then, says that he thinks that in his family his father was the final arbiter on all matters of importance (to the family). In so doing, he is attributing a certain belief (viz., B2) to himself. Although we might ordinarily say that what he thereby does is to tell us what he believes, I wish to keep clear the distinction between one's *asserting* that one has a particular belief and one's *asserting* that particular belief, on the one hand, and one's *having* that particular belief, on the other. To make this clear, I will talk of *asserting* (that one has) a belief, and of *having* (or *holding*) a belief, respectively.

Tim, then, has asserted that he holds this belief. I wish to leave open the question of whether he does in fact hold that belief. The main reason for this is that I assume that one's assertion of a particular belief is one bit of evidence for the claim that he in fact holds that belief, but is not, however, the only evidence. Nor is it always conclusive or without overriding counter-evidence. That is, sometimes a person claims to have a certain belief and in spite of that, we have such overwhelmingly strong evidence that he does not have that belief, that we conclude that his claim (that he has that belief) is false (from which it does *not* follow, of course, that he is lying). We conclude, that is, not that the belief itself is false, but that the individual's claim to have that belief is false. (We conclude that the individual does not in fact hold that belief.)

How, then, can we explain Tim's asserting that he thinks that his father was the final arbiter on all matters of importance to the family, i.e., his asserting that he holds B2? Here, of course, we feel little compulsion to model this after the phenomenon of perception. But what can we say other than that suggested by such a model?

We can best begin by taking a somewhat obvious point into consideration. To repeat what I have just said above, one's asserting (that he holds) some belief is to be distinguished from one's actually holding that belief. It is nonetheless to be considered as evidence for his holding the belief. His doing so, then, may perhaps be explained by his holding that belief, but in any case, if what I have said above is correct, then such assertions are to be considered as manifestations of *some* belief or beliefs (and wants), but not necessarily of the belief which the individual in question is asserting (that he has).

If this is so, then we are in fact in need of no entirely *new* framework to explain the self-attribution of beliefs, but can show how this is a special case of an action (viz., that of making some assertion) which can be explained in terms of one's beliefs, wants, etc. Let us see how we can expand what we have already said about the manifestations of beliefs in order to account for this phenomenon of the self-attribution of beliefs.

In what follows, it will be important to distinguish quite clearly between each of the following: the belief that p, the judgment that p, the asserting that p, the belief that one believes that p, the judgment that one believes that p, etc., where each 'p' is replaced by some one declarative sentence. Below we will attempt to illuminate some of the interrelations between these.

These distinctions suggest the following. The action of asserting that one believes that p is different (conceptually distinguishable) from the action of asserting that p. As might be expected, the explanation given to explain (a particular case of) one's asserting that p will differ from the explanation of the parallel action of self-ascribing the belief that p. In this context, note that in discussing Tim and B2, below, we will attempt to explain his asserting that he believes B2, and *not* his asserting B2.

We will presently answer the question of how one comes to ascribe beliefs to oneself. In answering this, we will provide a general framework within which we will then reconsider the case of Tim and B2. Then we will employ this framework in answering the (second) question of how one is so usually correct in the self-attribution of beliefs.

In doing this, there are several points to be made. The first of these is to introduce a distinction not yet explicitly made. This distinction will then be used to introduce several claims about the generation and manifestation of beliefs, and to answer, finally, both of the questions before us.

To make this distinction explicit, let us consider a very short example. Laura believes (correctly) that her name is Laura. She also believes (correctly) that her roommate's name is Cindy. We ask Laura, not yet knowing her, what her name is. She replies that it is Laura. In giving an explanation of her reply, we call upon her first belief (viz., the belief that her name is Laura), but not on the other one. In this case, we take it that her first belief was relevant to her giving the reply she did, but that her second was not. We hold the first to have been partially efficacious in bringing about her comment, but not the second. (I am trying to avoid claiming that the first was *causally* responsible for her answer, since I think that the present problem can be worked out without first having to consider the problem of causal versus non-causal factors, explanations, etc.) In such a case as this, i.e., in cases in which a given belief would be called upon in bringing us to an explanation of a given phenomenon, was partially efficacious in bringing about that phenomenon,, etc., I will talk of that belief as being *operant*. Otherwise, that belief will be considered to be *non-operant*. This distinction will help us in our presentation of an explanation of the self-attribution of beliefs, in general, and of Tim's assertion, in particular.

We are now in a position to present a brief discussion of beliefs being operant or non-operant in the generation of other beliefs, including, most importantly, beliefs about one's own beliefs. This will then be presupposed in both of the answers to be given below. To do this, I will attempt to make a general point, to which I will then relate the questions at hand.

The point in focus here is that beliefs are capable of generating certain other beliefs. Differently stated, in some situations individuals come to have a certain belief because they have had certain other beliefs.[22] I assume that this general point is part of our common-sense, non-formalized theory involving such psychological concepts as beliefs, wants, etc. The thesis relevant to our problem, which will be presented directly below, is just a more limited instance of this general point.

Our thesis, then is that having certain beliefs may result in having certain other beliefs, related to the first beliefs in certain specific ways. Our present problem is to make explicit the specific relations involved between resultant and effective (operant) beliefs.

We can make explicit the relations mentioned above in the following way.[23] Suppose that a given conjunction of beliefs, Bg (to suggest "generating beliefs"), *establishes* a belief Br (to

---

[22]As a simple example: We tell George that Lope de Vega was born in 1562. He then asks us when Lope died. We explain this as follows. Our telling George about Lope leads George to believe b1, that Lope was born in 1562. Having this belief, perhaps together with the belief b2, that no one born that long ago would be still alive, brought about George's having b3, that Lope is dead. Wanting to know when Lope died and believing that we would tell him if he asked, he asked us his question. Here, then, we have an example of one belief, b1 (or perhaps the two beliefs, b1 and b2) generating another belief, b3.

[23]What follows should be compared with the analysis of Hempel's: "Let us say that a person is a *consciously rational agent* (at a certain time) if (at that time) his actions are rational relative to those of his objectives and beliefs which he consciously takes into account in arriving at his decision." ("Rational Action," *Proceedings and Addresses of The American Philosophical Association,* vol. 35 (October, 1962), p. 21, his emphases.)

suggest "resultant belief"). (Bg establishes Br if and only if either Bg entails that Br or it is highly probable on the basis of Bg that Br.) Given this, we can state our thesis as: A given conjunction of beliefs Bg can generate a resultant belief Br if Bg establishes that Br.[24]

If we restate this, using the notion of operant beliefs already introduced, we can say that if, in a given case of beliefs generating new beliefs, the conjunction of operant beliefs Bg establishes (in the above-defined sense) Br, then the belief which *can* thereby be generated is Br.

To take a specific case of the above, we have the following. If one has a Bg which establishes that one believes that p, then Bg, if operant in generating new beliefs, can generate the belief that one believes that p. And this, please note, is a belief about one's own beliefs.

It is now appropriate to discuss in detail (1) how a belief about one's own beliefs can come about, be generated, and, (2) how such a belief can manifest itself. After this general discussion, we will consider the case of Tim and B2.

Let us assume that a given individual, A, has beliefs, B_A. As stated in the introductory chapter and earlier in this chapter, this B_A can manifest itself in various ways, e.g., by being operant in A's judging (any, several, or all parts of) B_A to be true, in A's asserting (any, &c., of) B_A, and in other behavior and thoughts. Let us refer to the manifestations of B_A as Man (B_A).

It is both essentially important and interesting to realize that Man (B_A) can itself generate beliefs. (For example: A mani-

---

[24]In the preceding footnote giving the case of George's belief about Lope de Vega, e.g., Bg consists of beliefs b1 and b2, viz., b1: Lope de Vega was born in 1562, and b2: No person born in 1562 would be alive today, and Br is the belief that Lope de Vega is dead.

To take a different example: Bg is b1-b3, viz., b1: John Cage considers the role that silence plays in music to be of extreme importance, or, in short, John Cage considers silence to be musically golden, b2: Almost all of Cage's views on music, especially the ones most central to his aesthetics of music, are worth serious consideration, and, b3: The role of silence in music is essential to Cage's aesthetics of music, and Br is the belief that the claim that silence is musically golden is worth serious consideration.

fests his belief that there is still some cold beer in the refrigerator by walking toward the refrigerator (in order to get a beer). In so doing, this manifestation generates the belief (in A) that A is walking toward the refrigerator.) Generally stated, the beliefs which can thereby be generated are beliefs that one has just performed certain actions, had certain thoughts, etc. [which are, in fact, manifestations of B_A]. We can abbreviatedly refer to these beliefs as B (Man (B_A)). Differently stated, manifestations of a given belief can be operant in generating the belief that certain phenomena came about. [These being, in fact, manifestations of B_A.]

But the claim that actions, thoughts, etc. (which are, in fact, manifestations of a given belief) obtained is itself supporting grounds for the claim that one has manifested the given belief, and, *a fortiori*, for the claim that one has this given belief. That is, given that one accepts certain statements asserting that one has performed certain actions, had certain thoughts, etc. (which are, in fact, all manifestations of some belief), one has grounds for accepting both (1) the claim that one has *manifested* that belief, and, (2) the claim that one *has* that (manifested) belief.

This is the framework within which we will explain how one comes to have beliefs about one's beliefs. We can now say, by way of summation, that one comes to have beliefs about one's own beliefs by beliefs about one's behavior, about the having of thoughts (judgments, free associatons, and other PPEs), etc. generating beliefs which can serve to explain why such behavior, thoughts, etc. came about. This, of course, does *not* require us to say that any conscious process of ratiocination or hypothesis-consideration (for the purpose of explaining this behavior, etc.) took place. We may hold, to be supported below, that these pieces of behavior, thoughts, etc., may well be the manifestations of the beliefs that the individual himself holds that he has.

This, then, provides a framework in which to explain the genesis of beliefs about one's own beliefs. When we turn our attention to the question of assertions or judgments (not held to be equivalent) about one's own beliefs, we should realize that beliefs about one's beliefs are just a species of belief. As such, the central characterizations we hold to belong to beliefs also belong to them. For (one, short) example, if we consider our statement Tg from the first chapter:

> (Tg) If x believes that p, then under favorable conditions, and unless there are some factors which prevent that belief from being manifested in the judgment that p, x will, upon considering whether or not p, judge that p (is the case).

and consider the case in which p is that he (himself) has a given belief, we have Th:

> (Th) If x believes that he believes that s, then, under favorable conditions, and unless there are some factors which prevent that belief from being manifested in the judgment that he (x) believes that s, x will, upon considering whether or not he believes that s, judge that he believes that s.

This, then, expresses just one of the ways in which beliefs about beliefs can manifest themselves. If we take into account the fact that this kind of belief can manifest itself in ways parallel to those in which other kinds of beliefs do, we can now address ourselves to the case of Tim's asserting that he holds B2. In order for us to explain this action,[25] we have to introduce more information about Tim.

Let us add, then, that when Tim was a child, many matters which immediately affected his family and which they considered to be important were discussed by the parents. All of the children were allowed to listen and add to the discussion. Furthermore, let us imagine that Tim's father talked at great length during these discussions. But let us also suppose that

---

[25]Notice that by now we have explicity rejected perception as the model most adequate for illuminating the phenomenon of self-ascription of beliefs and replaced that model by the model of action (the model of doing something).

many of these long comments were followed by rather strong criticisms and also counter-suggestions by Tim's mother.

Given this information, we can begin to give an explanation of Tim's making his assertion of holding B2 by first seeing which beliefs such a background will provide someone with. (These will be numbered for ease of reference later.) Such events in his childhood as mentioned above, then, have generated in Tim the beliefs that:

(B3) Many matters of importance to the family were discussed by the family.

(B4) (Tim's) father made long authoritative comments on the topics of discussion at such meetings.

(B5) (Tim's) father spoke much more than did (his) mother at these meetings.

Further, we know the context in which Tim did what he did, i.e., asserted that he holds B2. Knowing this context, we can also attribute belief B6 to Tim:

(B6) Comments about the family power structure of the home in which one grew up are extremely relevant to the conversation being held.

That Tim holds this belief could be explained on the basis of our sketchy general statements about belief generation (acquisition) together with certain facts about the particular circumstances of this example. But we are not primarily interested here in explaining the genesis of B6 but rather in explaining Tim's act of asserting that he holds B2.

We now further assume that Tim wants to contribute to the conversation (W1) and wants to project the image of having a strong male self-concept (W2). (Our reasons for assuming that Tim has these desires, *if* this were an actual case, might be Tim's attentive following of the conversation, his general enjoyment in partaking of conversations with these people, his lack of certainty about what kind of person these people think he is, his desire to be thought of by all as manly, etc., etc.) These wants, W1 and W2, together with B6, give us good reason to attribute to him the third want (W3) of wanting to make a comment relevant to the discussion of the family power structure in the home in which he grew up and the fourth want (W4) of wanting to comment about the manly image he accepts of his father (and thereby suggest that insofar as he identifies with his father he himself has a strong male self-concept). If needed, we can further explain our attributing these last two wants to Tim on the basis of the theoretical supposition Ti that if x believes that performing some action A is a way of doing D, and x wants to do D, then, x will be more likely to want to perform that action A than otherwise, *ceteris paribus*. (This is rather similar to theoretical statement Td given in the first chapter and to (d) given on p. 427 of the Brandt and Kim article, *op. cit.*)

But we still have not fully explained how it is that Tim makes the comment that he does. In order to do this, we have to explain how he came to believe B7:

(B7) I (Tim) believe that father was the final arbiter on all matters of importance to the family.

that is, I (Tim) believe B2. Once we can attribute B7 to Tim, we can on the basis of that and our attribution of W3 and W4 to him, also attribute W5 to him:

(W5) Wanting to make the comment that he (Tim) thinks that his father was the final arbiter on all matters of importance to the family in which he grew up

viz., that he holds B2, what Tim *did* say. Once we have attributed B7, W3, W4, and W5 to Tim, we are in a position to explain his asserting B7, i.e., his asserting that he holds B2. We should now, therefore, explain just how Tim has come to believe B7.

In order to explain how Tim came to believe B7, we are in need of the framework developed above in discussing the general problem of how one comes to have beliefs about one's own beliefs.

In applying the conclusions of our general discussion to this case, we will primarily make use of the notions of manifestations of beliefs in the generation of new beliefs, etc., and of the notion of one conjunction of beliefs establishing (in the above-discussed sense) another belief.

We can now make the following points. First, beliefs B3-B5 establish B2, and, therefore, can generate B2. Further, beliefs B3-B5, and B2, can be operant in bringing about Tim's making certain judgments, performing certain actions, etc., viz., in their manifestations, Man (B2), . . . , Man (B5). As a brief aside, we can give as examples: the act of calling *his* (*Tim's*) wife and children together to discuss issues of importance, in an attempt at copying a home life he found to be healthy and invigorating (manifesting B3); the recalling, taken to be a kind of judgment, that in his (Tim's) family his father was the final arbiter on all matters of importance (manifesting B2), etc. And of course, such manifestations as these, viz., Man (B2), . . . , Man (B5), are capable of generating beliefs B (Man (B2)), etc. And these, in turn, establish B7, and are capable, therefore, of generating B7.

Why, then, it might be asked, should we claim that B2, intermediatary beliefs about manifestations of B2 and perhaps of B3-B5, and B7 have in fact been generated? What grounds, that is, do we have which might substantiate these claims? I think at this point we can put forth the following grounds. First, we have reason to attribute B3-5 to Tim. We can also show that B3-5 establish (in the above-defined sense) B2. Given this, together with the thesis I have put forth above about which beliefs might have been generated in given cases, it is possible that B2 has been generated. And given this, together with the assumption that any, several, or all of B2 and B3-5 have been manifested and thereby generated what I referred to above as beliefs about the manifestations of beliefs, i.e., B (Man (Bx)), it is possible that B7 has been generated. Furthermore, we have evidence for the claim that B7 has been generated. This evidence is the fact that Tim asserted that he holds B2 and that he has want W2.

The evidence amounts to there being an event which can be explained by Tim's having W5 and B7. There is, however, nothing viciously circular about this. The logic of the argument in support of the supposition that B7 has in fact been generated is that readily accepted in explanation of phenomena employing low level hypotheses in physical science.

Compare it, e.g., with the explanation of a bullet's falling to earth exactly 4927 feet from the end of the muzzle of the rifle out of which it was shot. We know that the bullet was travelling at an initial angle of 23° above the horizontal, and that it has a given average velocity in still air. By vectoral analysis of this velocity, we can determine its vertical component, and this information together with equations for rate of fall of objects near the surface of the earth allows us to determine how long it took the bullet to fall to earth. But given this we can also determine the actual average velocity that it must have had during its flight in order for it to have landed where it did. From the discrepency between this velocity and its average velocity in still air (as given to us on the basis of tests run in a laboratory by the ammunitions manufacturer), we can tell what the (vectoral value in the appropriate direction of the) average wind velocity must have been during the flight. Suppose that this is 2.3 m.p.h.

In this example, then, the logic of the argument in support of the supposition that B7 has been generated is that of the argument in support of the supposition that the average wind velocity was 2.3 m.p.h. In each case we have independent evidence for each of the other claims involved. Furthermore, we have reason in each case to assume that what is claimed to have obtained *might* have obtained. Finally, accepting the supposition allows us to explain how what is to be explained did obtain, whereas not accepting it leaves us without an explanation. And in both cases there are ways (independent of determining whether the event being explained obtained) which might have been employed to determine whether what is claimed to have obtained did in fact come about.

It is extremely important, however, to make clear in what ways the two cases differ. In the case of the common-sense theory embodying the concept of belief (and that of wanting, etc.), we have only a very rough notion of what factors determine whether or not a given belief which can be generated by a given set of beliefs *will* in a given case be generated. This is in part responsible for the fact that most if not all of the natural sciences contain more adequate theories than this common-sense theory. I assume that determining what these factors are is *part* of the work of any psychological (and perhaps of any psychiatric) theory which attempts to incorporate and codify our ordinary psychological concepts (such as that of belief). I also take it that such problems as this one are among the most difficult and interesting of those involving these concepts. A mentalistic theory which provides us with explanations as to why certain beliefs were generated (as opposed to *not* being generated, or as opposed to *others* having been generated) is for that reason more illuminating than it would have been had it left this unexplained.[26]

We have explained, then, Tim's performing the action of asserting that he holds B2. We have done this by appeal to how certain operant beliefs (and wants. etc.) can manifest themselves. One of these ways is that of asserting something to be the case. It is because one has a given set of operant beliefs (and perhaps wants) that anyone asserts in given contexts that he has a given belief b_i. The above case of Tim's asserting that he holds B2 is such a case of operant beliefs (and wants) bringing it about that a certain assertion is made.

This leaves us with the other questions raised at the beginning of this chapter and in the subsequent discussion, viz., those of how it is that one is so often correct in the self-ascription of beliefs and of why we hold this self-ascription to have such warrant. We are now ready to answer these two.

---

[26]In Sartre's explanation of what he calls "bad faith" (in *Being and Nothingness, op. cit.*), he presents an explanation which he claims is adequate yet which does not employ the Freudian notion of the unconscious. He takes bad faith to be partially a result of *merely* having failed to have drawn certain conclusions, or, in other words, for some of his beliefs *merely* to have failed to generate certain other beliefs which they might have. As a Freudian theory explains what Sartre assumed as inexplicable (as "brute" facts), it is for that reason more, not less, acceptable than the Sartrean model.

Let us first consider the question of why one is so often correct in the self-ascription of beliefs. One is correct in a self-ascription of a belief, of course, if someone ascribes the belief that s to himself and it is the case that he believes that s. One is so often correct in the self-ascription of beliefs because it is so often the case that the belief that s has been operant (through the intermediary of its manifestations, Man (Bs)) in generating beliefs which can manifest themselves in the assertion (or, alternatively, in the judgment) that one believes that s. (See the presentation of the general framework within which this point is being made, above.) Such a belief which might have been generated by Man (Bs) is, for example, the belief that one believes that s. More will be said on this matter directly below, in considering the question of the warrant of self-ascriptions of belief.

At this point we can turn to the question of what warrant the individual has in self-ascribing beliefs, and at the same time, clarify what important differences (and similarities) there are between A's claim that A has a given belief and B's claim that A has a given belief.

At a given time, A judges that he (A) has a given belief. He can do this, of course, without considering what he has thought or how he has behaved in the past. Let us suppose, further, that B too judges that A has this given belief. He too can do this without considering what A has thought or how A has behaved in the past.

When we consider A's judging that he (A) has the belief that s, we can explain this judgment by assuming that A has the belief in question, i.e., the belief that s. We can hypothesize, that is, that A's belief that s is operant in bringing about thoughts (and PPEs) and/or behavior which in turn generate beliefs which themselves can bring about the belief that A (himself) believes that s.

We assume, that is, that an adequate explanation of A's coming to believe that he (A) believes that s will almost surely include mention of A's believing that s.

Supporting this supposition is the following: an individual has the opportunity to gather much more information (beliefs) about his own behavior and thoughts (as PPEs) than anyone else. As a result of this, it is much less likely that he be incorrect about hypotheses concerning his own beliefs than others are about them. For he is in a position to collect information concerning more judgments (this at least partly because one can judge silently, i.e., without speaking aloud) and of much more behavior (this because one is sometimes or often alone) than anyone else.

This suggests, first of all, that the kind of evidence which A has to call upon upon which to base claims concerning his own beliefs is of the same sort available to others. That is, what A can observe is what can be taken to be the direct manifestation of A's beliefs. But others are in this same epistemological position with reference to A's beliefs. That is, A is in a position to come to have the belief that he (A) believes that s in virtue of his knowledge of his part behavior, assertions, judgments, free associations, etc. But this is exactly how others come to have beliefs about what A's beliefs are, viz.: on the basis of what might be manifestations of A's belief that s they come to believe that A believes that s.

This same point also suggests that this epistemological priority is one of degree rather than one of kind. It also suggests that others, by being with A continuously for many years, might come to have grounds on which to base or justify claims that A's beliefs which approach those available to A himself.

This, then, is our answer to the last of the questions raised in the first part of this chapter. We have come to the conclusion that the warrant given to one's assertion that one has a given belief is not based on any logical interconnection between such assertions and related beliefs.

This warrant is based, rather, on the fact that individuals have a huge inventory of information about themselves on which to base claims about their beliefs. We hold it to be rather unlikely that they will draw unreasonable (on the basis of the total information available to them) conclusions about what their beliefs are,[27] but this is a psychological rather than a logical point: And, it might be stated, it is not *so* unlikely when, e.g., their self-concept is at stake.

Before we leave this discussion, there are several notions I think we can now illuminate on the basis of what we have already said. First of all, we can see that the concepts of reasonableness and of insightfulness can be analyzed, at least partially, utilizing our notions of operant and non-operant beliefs in the generation of new beliefs.

Being insightful, for example, consists (at least partially) in actually having beliefs generated on the basis of relatively few beliefs which provide rather deep understanding of the original beliefs. Paraphrased into less technical language, this amounts to saying that the insightful individual is one who realizes on the basis of little evidence what a certain phenomenon amounts to, who realizes on that basis that a certain phenomenon can be structured in a certain way which provides an understanding of that phenomenon. For example, one exhibits insightfulness if one sees very little of a stranger's behavior but nonetheless realizes that the stranger is a very kind yet strong person, is full of self-confidence but is not haughty, etc., etc. Seeing the stranger for one brief moment, and thereby coming to have beliefs about what he (the stranger) is doing, the individual who is insightful thereby also comes to have beliefs which provide an understanding of much about this stranger's character, etc. (The insightful individual sees much in very little.) (Inso-

---

[27]Note that we have held here that knowledge of beliefs is not part of the beliefs themselves, but a matter involving much self-awareness. In this way we hint that the basic question is not how someone might be in ignorance of his beliefs but rather how one is in any case *not* ignorant of them. This is parallel to the point made powerfully in extended discussion by my friend Robert Solomon. See his *Unconscious Motivation*, Doctoral Thesis, University of Michigan, Department of Philosophy, December, 1967.

Similarly, Brenner (*op. cit.*) has claimed that a fundamental hypothesis of psychoanalytic theory is "that consciousness is an exceptional rather than a regular attribute of psychic processes" (p. 2), "that psychic activity is principally unconscious," i.e., nonconscious. (p. 33).

far as intelligence is *partially* composed of insightfulness, this illuminates a little of that notion.)

Being reasonable (in the sense used in talking of making a rational decision on a given "information-basis", as proposed[28] by Hempel), amounts to generating only those beliefs which can be generated on the basis of one's whole corpus of beliefs, or, more precisely, only those beliefs which would be generated on the basis of *all* relevant beliefs.

Most importantly, we can analyze the notion of an unconscious belief given this framework. An unconscious belief, Bu, is one such that the individual will not (cannot) have the judgment generated either that Bu or that it would be correct to ascribe to himself the belief Bu, but which manifests itself (i.e., Bu) in (perhaps many) other ways.[29]

As an aside, the above analyses suggest a parallel analysis of the notion of an unconscious want, viz., that an unconscious want, Wu, is one such that the individual will not (cannot) have the judgment generated that it would be correct to ascribe Wu to himself, but which manifests itself (i.e., Wu) in (perhaps many) other ways.[30]

Before presenting several cases of unconscious beliefs from psychiatric literature in order to show where my analysis of unconscious beliefs is applicable, let us consider the following. It has been said that "the difference between A's consciously wanting P and B's unconsciously wanting P comes down to a difference in the way they are disposed to treat certain explanations (and descriptions) of their behavior."[31] This seems to amount to the following: B who unconsciously wants P will refuse to accept

---

[28]*Aspects of Scientific Explanation* (New York, The Free Press, 1966), p. 464.

[29]This is not to say that this individual can *never* judge either that Bu or that he holds Bu. For Bu may at some later time change its status and no longer be an unconscious belief (through psychoanalysis, intense self-scrutiny, drugs, etc.) Cf. the following footnote.

[30]This is not to say that this individual can *never* judge that he hold Wu. For Wu may at some later time no longer be an unconscious want. Cf. the preceding footnote.

[31]Wm. Henninger, "The Logical Structure of Unconscious Motives" (Ann Arbor, Michigan, 1966, mimeograph), p. 9.

or offer explanations or descriptions of his behaviour in terms
of his wanting P. That is, he will reject explanations and descriptions of his behavior which presuppose that he wants P. If
what I have just given as an analysis of unconscious wants is
correct, the above (Henninger) claim reveals a central characteristic of unconscious motives, but a characteristic which can
itself be explained in terms of a more basic characteristic. That
is, given my analysis, it follows that an individual with a given
unconscious want will not judge that he has that want. Since
this is so, it follows that he will not judge that any of his behavior is explicable in terms of that want, since to do so would
be to require one (logically) to accept the claim that one has
that want. Given our analysis, the facts in focus in the Henninger claim follow. (The Henninger claim, that is, can be seen as
just one consequent of our more general analysis.)

We can now briefly consider some of the cases of unconscious belief discussed in the literature. Freud, for example,
talks of the operation of certain superstitious beliefs which are
nonetheless denied access to consciousness. He holds, that is,
that certain beliefs are held by the individual, do manifest
themselves in various ways, but which are such that the individual will never judge that he possesses them: "our parapraxes
make it possible for us to practise all those pious and superstitious customs that must shun the light of consciousness, owing
to opposition from our reason, which has now grown skeptical."[32]
Freud also talks of the "symbolic mode of expression" which
a dreamer employs yet "does not know in waking life and does
not recognize." He takes it that "the knowledge of symbolism
is unconscious to the dreamer, that it belongs to his unconscious mental life."[33]

In two early papers, Freud talks of a "repressed memory" (a
memory being a particular kind of belief),[34] and of amnesias,

---

[32]*The Standard Edition of the Complete Psychological Works of Freud*,
vol. 6, trans. A. Tyson (London, The Hogarth Press, Ltd., and The
Institute of Psycho-analysis, 1963), p. 175.

[33]*Ibid.*, vol. 15, trans. J. Strachey, p. 165.

[34]"Further Remarks on the Defense Neuro-psychoses," *Collected Papers*,
op. cit., vol. 1, p. 164.

which are held to be the result of the process of repression.[35] In this second article, amnesias are considered to be gaps in memory, the filling in of which is said to be in "essence equivalent" to having "all repressions . . . undone; . . . in making the unconscious accessible to consciousness."[36]

Reik discusses the case of a man who unconsciously believes that there is a God and that He will hurt him (if he has sexual intercourse with a certain woman), even though he consciously professes to be an atheist.[37]

Brill talks of a man who lost a knife given to him by his wife. He was afraid of losing her and "unconsciously believed that a donated knife may cut friendship between the persons concerned. . . .[B]y sacrificing the knife he made the superstitious ban impotent."[38]

Devereux claims that "[u]nconsciously in our society, . . . the illegitimate child is imagined to be an incestuous child."[39]

And Pedersen claims that experiences "relevant to the self which are repressed are likely to be organized into an unconscious self-concept. There is evidence that characteristics unconsciously assigned to the self may be quite discrepant from those consciously assigned to the self."[40]

Other examples are, of course, available from the literature, but my purpose here has been merely to show the applicability of the concept of unconscious beliefs.

[35]"Freud's Psycho-analytic Method," *Collected Papers, op. cit.,* vol. 1, p. 267.

[36]*Ibid,* p. 269.

[37]*Listening with the Third Ear: The Inner Experience of a Psychiatrist* (New York, Grove Press, 1948), pp. 338-341.

[38]Cited in the Brill translation of Freud's *Psychopathology of Everyday Life* (New York, Mentor Books, 1964), p. 116. (Interestingly enough, the case does not appear in the German original, *Zur Psychopathologie des Alltagslebens,* vierte Auflage (Berlin, Verlag von S. Karger, 1912), even in this fourth edition which is supposedly the basis of the Brill translation.

[39]"Anthropological Data Suggesting Unexplored Attitudes toward and in Unwed Mothers," *Archives of Criminal Psychodynamics,* vol. 1 (1965) p. 574.

[40]"Ego Strength and Discrepancy between Conscious and Unconscious Self-Concepts," *Perceptual and Motor Skills,* vol. 20, No. 3, part 1 (1965), p. 691.

This, then, concludes our answer to the first of the two problems mentioned at the beginning of this chapter about the self-attribution of beliefs, viz., how one can so readily, accurately, and with such "immediacy" ascribe or refuse to ascribe a belief to himself.

Before closing this chapter, however, there is one complex of questions which I have until this point carefully avoided introducing into our discussion in order that we might deal separately with it. I would now like to address this complex.

Up until now I have said nothing committal (with one exception that will be handled in the following pages) about whether *earnest* assertions of belief have a logical relation with the holding of the cited belief. I have, that is, avoided the question of whether 'A earnestly asserts that s.' entails 'A believes that s.' Since the same basic problem arises in questioning the relation between judging and believing, I have also avoided the question of whether 'A judges that s.' entails 'A believes that s.'

The one exception to this noncommitment is my mentioning at the beginning of this chapter the (putative) example of one who earnestly asserts that he thinks that all people are equal yet who has a prejudice against Orientals. I suggested there that this is one type of case of one who makes a non-deceitful self-ascription of a given belief to whom *we* nonetheless refuse to ascribe that belief. We will return to this below.

I was at one time of the opinion that it was not necessary to construe 'A judges that s.' as entailing 'A believes that s.' The considerations in virtue of which I substantiated this position no longer seem tenable to me. Below I will consider two alternative ways in which to understand such cases as mentioned above (cases of self-deception). In the first alternative, A1, the first statement (about judging) is not held to entail the second (about believing), while in the second, A2, it is. More precise formulations of A1 and A2 appear below.

Let us return in this context to what we take to be cases of self-deception, which for the moment we can continue to characterize as cases in which we hold both that the self-deceiver thinks that he has a given belief, and also that he in fact does not have that belief. If such an individual were questioned about the truth of that belief he would of course hold it to be true. Why is this so?

If in a given situation one judges that he believes that s, if he is questioned about s itself, he will obviously hold s to be true. (For example: I believe that cats are calmer creatures than dogs. (The preceding can be construed as my expressing a judgment of mine about one of my beliefs.) I now ask myself whether cats are calmer creatures than dogs. It is not surprizing that I now think, i.e., judge, that they are.) This consideration suggests the following:

(Tj) If x believes that he believes that s, then, under favorable conditions, and unless there are some factors which prevent that belief from being manifested in the judgment that s, x will, upon considering whether or not s, judge that s.

(Note that unlike Th, Tj is not simply a particular case of Tg.) If in a given case we explain one's judging that s by calling upon Tj and not upon Tg, we have explained one's judging that s without supposing that he believes that s. The importance of this is that it allows us to maintain the position that 'A judges that s.' and 'A earnestly asserts that s.' do not, either singly or jointly, entail 'A believes that s.' Recall that this was what is essential to A1. In what follows I will take A1 to be that alternative supplementation of Ta-Ti consisting of Tj alone (obviously excluding Tk-Tn, introduced below).

Below I will suggest an alternative way of construing the phenomenon of self-deception, one involving acceptance of A2. In this 'A judges that s.' and 'A earnestly asserts that s.' both, either singly or jointly, entail 'A believes that s.' This will of course require us to say that all individuals in self-deception who make judgments or earnest assertions about relevant beliefs have mutually inconsistent beliefs.

To be explicit, A2 will consist of Tk-Tn, introduced below. What will be important in the following discussion is that supplementing Ta-Ti with A2 will allow for a structuring and an understanding of certain relevant phenomena left unstructured and inexplicable by rejecting A2. Since this is what I take to be important, I will not address the question of whether Tj is of itself acceptable, nor will I attempt to arbitrate between A2 and, say, an A3 consisting of Tj-Tn. (Of course there are alternative supplementations of Ta-Ti not identical to either A1 or A2.)

Since A1 allows one to avoid claiming that certain individuals (those who judge that s yet believe that not-s) hold inconsistent beliefs (at least insofar as they make this judgment and have this belief), and since it might be held that this is an advantage for a theory of belief, let me add the following.

It seems obvious that a given individual may have two sets of beliefs S1 and S2 such that these two are inconsistent without the belief-possessor realizing that they are inconsistent beliefs, whether or not we hold that judging entails believing (speaking loosely about entailment for the moment), our position on the former issue does not depend on our position on the latter. (This consideration detracts from the initial preferability of the first alternative to the second.)

More importantly, in cases of self-deception, there are certain patterns of behavior, of conclusion-drawing, of judgment, etc. which bear a particular relation to the (unconscious) belief in question. I think that this can be best understood by postulating a belief contradictory to the unconscious belief, which for reasons which will become obvious I propose to call a reactive belief.

In virtue of these considerations, let me introduce the following:

(Tk) If x judges that s, x believes that s.
(Tl) If x earnestly asserts that s, x believes that s.

We can introduce the notion of a reactive belief into the theory with:

(Tm) If x judges that s, x believes that not-s, and not-s is

>an unconscious belief, then x believes that s, and s is a reactive belief.
>
>(Tn) If x earnestly asserts that s, x believes that not-s, and not-s is an unconscious belief, then x believes that s, and s is a reactive belief.

Typical of a reactive belief is that there are adequate grounds in the given case for the ascription of the contradictory (unconscious) belief and yet the reactive belief itself is manifested in the related judgment (the belief that s in the judgment that s), in deliberate decisions and judgments based upon whether or not s, and in acts resultant from such decisions and judgments.

In saying this I do not want to give the impression that I think that it is always or even usually the case that one can state whether a reactive or the related unconscious belief will be the one to be manifested. In fact, this is simply one more instance (cf. the comments at the close of the example of the bullet falling to earth) in which it becomes obvious that we do not have a complete understanding of the workings of the mind.[41]

One can also note in this context that it is even possible at times for several of different relevant beliefs all to have certain manifestations within a short period of time.[42]

---

[41]Cf. "The greatest defect of classical philosophy of mind, both rationalist and empiricist, seems to me to be its unquestioned assumption that the properties and content of the mind are accessible to introspection; it is surprising to see how rarely this assumption has been challenged, insofar as the organization and function of the intellectual faculties are concerned, even with the Freudian revolution." N. Chomsky, *Language and Mind* (N.Y., Harcourt, Brace & World, Inc. 1958), p. 22.

[42]An example of this: The relevant beliefs are all (different) beliefs about what the situation in which one finds himself amounts to. Each of these is serially manifested in the judgment that the situation is such-and-such. (Again, each judgment different, as were the beliefs in question.) With each of these judgments, the individual sees his immediately previous way of reacting to the situation as inappropriate, and abruptly changes how he is acting. (Judgments often have an immediate effect on how one then acts.) Note that such changes, e.g., from laughing to sitting calmly to questioning what time it is to crying to . . ., can be seen at one time

The above-introduced notion of reactive beliefs is designed, inter alia, to provide a framework in which to understand such cases as the following. Ann thinks that her father is cruel and unloving toward her (belief B8). B8 is an unconscious belief. This belief generates resentment which in turn generates the desires to punish and to estrange her father (W6 and W7). Ann also has certain beliefs about what would count as punishing or estranging her father. Let us for simplicity refer to them collectively as B9. These wants (W6 and W7) together with this belief (B9) are manifested in hostile acts, which are of course manifestations, viz., Man(W6, W7, B9). Particular manifestations Man (W6, W7, B9) are seen as [43] manifestations of certain relevant beliefs and of the desire to establish independence from her family (W8), of the desire to be with others (W9), as opposed to, for example, the desire to leave her father alone and lonely (W10), and so forth. *Some* Man (W6, W7, B9) are not understood by Ann at all. Some, that is, are seen by Ann as acting oddly, "out of character", as if something "came over her", etc. In addition, whenever anything which might be a manifestation of B8 is considered by Ann, she does not see it as a Man(B8). (All of these judgments about these manifestations would/can be explained employing the assumption that Ann has the belief contradictory to B8, reactive belief B10.)

At this point it might be interesting to relate the preceding

---

(by the person himself) as actions *becoming* appropriate to the situation and, ironically, also (by another, e.g., a psychiatrist) as inconsistent and inappropriate.

Contrast J. Perceval, *Perceval's Narrative* (G. Bateson, ed., Stanford, Stanford University Press, 1961), Chap. 8, p. 32: "On my way, I was tormented by the commands of what I imagined was the Holy Spirit. . . . These contradictory commands were the cause, now, as before, of the incoherency of my behavior."

[43]Cf. Sartre, *The Transcendence of the Ego,* op. cit., p. 76: "When I unify my consciousness under the title "hatred," I add a certain meaning to them, I qualify them." Sartre previously stated (p. 75) that one may be mistaken about such matters: "I can see clearly that I am ill-tempered, jealous, etc., and nonetheless I may be mistaken. In other words, I may deceive myself." (Note this use of "seeing that s" in which s may nonetheless be false. Cf. footnote 28 of chapter 1.)

to some of the parallel discussions in psychiatric literature, especially in Freud's writings. Recall that the relevant notion of impossibility in discussions by Freud and others of the impossibility of an unconscious belief's manifesting itself in the related judgment is explicated in terms of repression.[44]

Brenner explicitly states "that we don't know for sure whether there is any type of forgetting other than repression.[45] He also states the human mind has a "usually unsuspected capacity . . . for forgetting, or, more precisely, for repressing."[46]

Elsewhere Freud's discussion suggests that repression comes about because of one's need to have a certain self-concept. (Reconsider here the Pedersen article cited above.)

> Repression, as we have said, proceeds from the ego; we might have said with greater precision: from the self-respect of the ego.[47]
>
> From the point of view of the ego this formation of an ideal would be the condition of repression.[48]

---

[44]See, for example, "Repression," *Collected Papers, op. cit.*, vol. 4, p. 86. Cf. the discussion below in footnote 48.

[45]Op. cit., p. 89, my italics. See also the text, above, to which footnotes 34-36 refer.

[46]*Ibid.*, p. 143.

[47]"On Narcissism: An Introduction," in *Collected Papers, op. cit.*, vol. 4, p. 50. Cf. F. Nietzsche, *Beyond Good and Evil* (Trans. W. Kaufmann, N.Y., Random House Vintage Books, 1966), Part 4, Section 68. Contrast A. Schopenhauer, *The World as Will and Representation* (N.Y., Dover Publications, Inc., 1966), vol. 2, Supplements to the Third Book, ch. 32 ("On Madness").

[48]"On Narcissism: An Introduction," *op. cit.*, p. 51. Compare these last two quotations with Freud's comment that the "motivations" of repression are to be found "in feelings of 'pain' (*Unlust*)." ("Freud's Psycho-analytic Method," *op. cit.*, p. 267) The German concept of Unlust (also translated as "unpleasure") is perhaps more correctly understood as displeasure, aversion, repugnance, or disinclination than as pain. Given this, it might be reasonable to supplement such a notion of repression (one based on avoidance of Unlust) to allow for a more intelligible explanation of (some cases of) post-hypnotic suggestion. There seem to be cases of post-hypnotic suggestion, that is, in which (a) there is material kept from consciousness post-hypnotically yet (b) there is no prima facie reason to postulate any aversion or repugnance being avoided.

This suggests, for example, that we introduce a new notion of blocking

After formulating the above concept of reactive beliefs (without having a name for them) and their characteristics, I found two discussion on the role of repression particularly relevant to the consideration with which we have ended this chapter. In the first of these, Freud introduces the notion of reactive rein-

---

other than repression, as it is above described; or, alternatively, that we consider the above-described repression as Unlust-repression, which we might then supplement with (minimally) a second type of repression to account for cases such as those involving post-hypnotic suggestion in which there seems to be no aversion or repugnance involved in there being material which cannot come to consciousness, which will not be judged by the possessor to be possessed by him.

Note that this prima facie need for supplementation of psychic processes arises even if we accept later suggestions by Freud (1926) "to re-adopt the old concept of defense if in doing so it is laid down that this shall be the general designation for all techniques of which the ego makes use in the conflicts which potentially lead to neurosis, while repression is the term reserved for one particular method of defense" (*The Problem of Anxiety*, tr. H. A. Bunker, N.Y., The Psychoanalytic Quarterly Press and W. W. Norton & Co., Inc., 1936, p. 144) and by Anna Freud (1936) that there are (at least?) ten methods of defense, ten defense mechanisms. (*The Ego and the Mechanisms of Defense*, tr. C. Baines, N.Y., International Universities Press, Inc., 1966, p. 47.)

For although the process of defense and that of repression *were* once (1896) held to be identical by Freud ("Further Remarks on the Defense Neuro-psychoses," *op. cit.*, p. 155, where he talks of "this psychical process of 'defense' or 'repression'"), in spite of his later claim (1937) that there "was never any doubt that repression was not the only method which the ego could employ for its purposes" ("Analysis Terminable and Interminable," *Collected Papers, op. cit.*, vol. 5, p. 338), these purposes previously being identified as "avoiding danger, anxiety and unpleasure" (*idem*), all defense mechanisms—whether repression is held to be the only kind of defense mechanism or one of a plurality of kinds—involve the avoidance of Unlust: "The purpose of the defense mechanisms is to avert dangers." ("Analysis Terminable and Interminable," *Collected Papers*, op. cit., vol. 5, p. 340. Cf. Anna Freud, *op. cit.*, p. 58, and her discussion, pp. 54-56, of suggestions made by Jeanne Lampl-de Groot and Helene Deutsch.)

This consideration strongly suggests that the problem raised above (suggesting a need for the supplementation mentioned) requires the postulation of some mechanism *not* based on the avoidance of Unlust, specifically, of some kind of blocking other than a defense mechanism. Note that at least some of the other nine defense mechanisms mentioned by Anna Freud, e.g., isolation, do not result in *any* unconscious material and are, therefore, simply irrelevant to this problem (even if they were *not* based on the avoidance of Unlust).

forcement and that of reactive thought. The latter notion can be seen as a formulation (already present in a psychiatric theory) of the notion I then called reactive beliefs (after Freud). Calling a train of thought which is incessantly repeated in consciousness exaggerated or reinforced, Freud remarks that:

> Contrary thoughts are always closely connected with each other and are often paired off in such a way that *the one thought is exaggeratedly conscious while its counterpart is repressed and unconscious.* . . . repression if often achieved by means of an excessive reinforcement of the thought contrary to the one which is to be repressed. This process I call *reactive* reinforcement, and the thought which asserts itself exaggeratedly in consciousness and . . . cannot be removed I call a *reactive thought.*[49]

This suggests that one way of understanding self-deception is to introduce into the theory of beliefs (and of mind) a concept of repression at least precise enough to involve something like what Freud calls reactive reinforcement. The result of such a process of repression and reactive reinforcement would be the presence of an unconscious belief s and of a reactive belief not-s. Thus, part of this might be expressed in the theory by

> (To) If x believes that s and s is an unconscious belief, then x believes that not-s, is a reactive belief, and vice versa.

(Note that To is not identical to Tm.) Given the preceding, we can also introduce the following:

---

[49]"Fragment of an Analysis of a Case of Hysteria," *Collected Papers, op. cit.*, vol. 3, pp. 67f., his emphases. As an aside, his comments in this paper about the similarity between reactive thoughts and prejudices might interestingly be compared with the S. Ferenczi article referred to in the first chapter. By a paper published three years later (1908), Freud had begun talking, no longer of reactive reinforcement, but of reaction-formations. ("Character and Anal Erotism," *Collected Papers, op. cit.*, vol. 2, p. 47.)

(Tp) If x believes that s and s is a reactive belief, x will, under favorable conditions, upon considering whether or not s, judge that s.

Self-deception on this model will be explained using Ta-Tp, and especially Tk-Tp. Rather importantly, we will have to revise our conception of self-deception. Central to this is seeing that our former insistence on denying that the self-deceiver believed what he asserted was based on our realization that what seemed *most* obvious was that he believed what was denied in his assertions. (His judgments on certain related issues, e.g., that Orientals are naturally slovenly, untrustworthy, cruel, inhuman, etc., his many relevant actions, etc., were all taken to be manifestations of this other belief. Note that the evidence for ascribing, in this example, the prejudice in question, includes verbal evidence. *It's not simply a matter of his words saying one thing and his actions another.*)

What was behind our insistence was what amounts to the position that reactive beliefs are not really beliefs at all. ("He doesn't really believe that!")

What I have tried to show is that there are grounds to show that reactive beliefs are ("really") beliefs, although perhaps of an odd kind. I think that reactive beliefs are at least as problematic as unconscious beliefs although much recent philosophy seems to find only the latter a problematic notion. Nonetheless I think that the introduction of both notions into the reconstruction and explication of a theory of beliefs is justified by the complexities (of human behavior, states, etc.) to be understood.

Self-deception, then, should be redescribed as a case in which an individual makes a self-ascription of a belief s, is not attempting to deceive others, yet holds that belief not-s, such that s is a reactive belief manifest in this judgment (and most likely elsewhere as well) and not-s is an unconscious belief.

In the second of the two discussions mentioned above, Freud discusses what can be described using the theoretical framework introduced in this chapter as the phenomenon in which in order to avoid coming to the judgment that s (where

s is an unconscious belief), one variously interprets manifestations of s (i.e., Man (Bs)) as manifestations of other beliefs or
perhaps sees these manifestations as incomprehensible, "out of
character":

> To begin with it may happen that an affect or emotion
> is perceived but misconstrued. By the repression of its
> proper representation it is forced to become connected
> with another idea, and is now interpreted by conscious-
> ness as the expression of this other idea.[50]

Although the wording here seems to suggest conceptual
misunderstandings on Freud's part about the nature of emotions,
if we interpret the presentation of something as its interpretation or import, an idea as a belief, the expression of an idea
as the manifestation of a belief, and the connection with an
idea as the association with a belief in one's (informal) theory
construction—all of which is at least plausible—Freud's description
amounts to an alternative formulation of one aspect of the
delineation of the dynamics involving unconscious and reactive
beliefs. To make this clearer consider the following restate-
ment along the above lines of Freud's description: To begin
with it may happen that an affect is perceived, but misconstrued.
By the repression of its proper interpretation or import, it is
forced to become associated with another belief, and now
interpreted as the manifestation of this other belief.

As I said at the beginning of the discussion of this second
alternative supplementation to the line of thought of this
chapter (A2), the choice between accepting A2 or not is to
be made on the basis of the facility with which hitherto
problematic issues could or could not be comprehended. Although further investigation into phenomena not encountered
in many armchair environments is relevant here, I have merely
wanted to give some hint of why I think that more extensive
considerations show accepting this second alternative to be
preferable to not accepting it. I find this line of theory con-

---

[50]"The Unconscious," *op. cit.*, p. 110.

struction more acceptable than remaining with what some might accept as the indeterminacy of ordinary notions. (At some points I choose to supplement conceptual analysis with conceptual explication.)

In the next chapter we will turn to a discussion of the second of the problems mentioned at the beginning of this chapter, viz., why comments relevant to a self-ascription of a belief are sometimes addressed to the correctness of the ascription and sometimes to the correctness of the belief.

CHAPTER III

THE PARENTHETICAL USE OF BELIEF CLAIMS

> "I carn't not believe this incredible
> fact of truth". John Lennon,
> *In His Own Write*, p. 18.

After the preliminary analysis of the concept of belief in the first chapter, we have been considering certain characteristics of belief in order to understand this concept more adequately. In the course of this activity we have addressed ourselves to the problem of providing an explanation of an individual's ability to make accurate self-ascriptions of beliefs, and of other related phenomena.

In the next chapters we will address another set of problems about this notion, viz., what the grounds are on which one can substantiate the claim that a given individual is the kind of thing which *can* have beliefs. For that purpose, we will concentrate on the particular question of whether robots can have beliefs.

Before turning to that, however, there is one contemporary analysis which might be taken to suggest that our entire analysis of belief is misguided. This analysis is one which suggests that when someone states that he believes that s, he is not doing what an analysis such as ours maintains that he is doing. He is, rather, informing the listeners of the degree to which he has confidence in the claim in question, viz., the claim that s. This suggests (A) that (the English) language would be less misleading if it always used a (sentential) modifier such as 'probably' or 'with some likelihood', rather than 'I believe (that)', and (B) that the verb 'believe' and the related noun 'belief' are what might be called grammatically misleading words.

If one takes this tack, one might be led to conclude that our entire enterprise is based essentially on a misunderstanding of belief-ascriptions, and, in particular, of what it is to claim to have a belief.

I think, however, that the insights of the type of analysis here referred to (to be presented below) can be accommodated within the framework of what we have already said. In this chapter we will try to do this. Let us consider the writings[1] in which certain twentieth century philosophers discuss certain phrases such as 'I believe', 'I'm certain', 'I know', etc. These philosophers suggest that the "parenthetical" verbs in these phrases have a radically different status than was previously supposed.

They give examples of certain first person singular uses of these verb phrases ('to believe', 'to be certain', 'to know')—also applicable to 'to be sure', 'to doubt', 'to hesitate to say', etc.— and contrast the situations in which one of them would be used with those in which the others would be used. Or more precisely, they contrast the situations in which certain sentences containing one would be used with those in which one of the others would be. We will call these first person singular uses "ego uses"; and the sentences or statements in which they appear "ego sentences" or "ego statements". All others will be called "non-ego uses", "non-ego sentences", etc.[2]

It was then noted that the speaker will get us to suppose that *he* has less confidence in his claim if he adds the parenthet-

---

[1]E.g., J. O. Urmson, "Parenthetical Verbs," *Mind*, vol. 61 (1952), pp. 192-212; J. L. Austin, "Other Minds," *Proceedings of the Aristotelian Society*, Supplementary Volume 20 (1946), pp. 148-187, esp. the section entitled "If I know I Can't Be Wrong"; L. Wittgenstein, *Philosophical Investigations*, trans. G. E. M. Anscombe (Oxford, Basil Blackwell, 1963), e.g., Part II, Section x (pp. 190ff.)

[2]Although what I will say below will not make explicit reference to first person *plural* uses of verb phrases (On the parallel of the term 'ego uses', these can be called "nos uses.") such as 'we believe', 'we know', 'we're sure', etc., these have rather interesting parallels to first person *singular* uses. (Classifying nos uses simply as non-ego uses will not tend to illuminate these parallels.)

ical phrase 'I believe' rather than 'I know', 'I'm sure', and vice versa, etc.

Furthermore, it was suggested that in some contexts the appropriate reply to a statement of the form 'I believe that s.' is *not* 'You really do (don't) believe that!', but rather 'It is true (false) that s.' (where each 's' is replaced by the same declarative sentence). Note in passing that if 'I believe that s.' is taken as equivalent, in some contexts, to 'With some likelihood, s.' or to 'Probably s.', it is obvious why one can relevantly respond addressing the question of the truth-value of s.

Some philosophers have concluded from these considerations that in at least some cases, to talk of believing or knowing something is not to report a mental event, a mental state, a mental happening, etc. Rather, it is said, these parenthetical phrases (in *some* contexts) serve quite a different function, viz.: to add in these cases that one is certain or believes is to indicate the degree to which he has confidence in the statement he is making. In those cases in which the parenthetical phrase is serving this function, we will talk of the "parenthetical use" of the phrase (or, of its verb).[3]

We have, then, the following problem: Whereas a "parenthetical verb" analysis of 'believe' does not (claim to) shed light on more general questions about belief, it seems that *our* account does not shed light on the parenthetical use of 'believe'. That is, if we are structuring behavior, thoughts, publically observable states, etc., of the individual in attributing a belief to him (as well as suggesting that certain explanations of his behavior, etc. will be correct), then why are (some) belief assertions treated as they are? That is, why is 'I believe that s.' sometimes *appropriately* countered by 'It's *not* the case that s!'? Similarly, but not equivalently, why are some utterance-instances of 'I believe that s.' correctly taken to be cases of guardedly stating that s? (Our analysis will have to be expanded to account for these facts.)

---

[3]Let me draw attention here to the fact that not all ego uses are parenthetical uses. (E.g., "I used to believe fervently that God would guarantee complete justice in the universe.")

Some ego uses of parenthetical verbs, then, allow for the possibility of two distinct types of relevant reply (in this context of considering 'I believe', one addressed to whether the belief is held; the other to whether what is believed is true). It is important to note that although this is so, this possibility is *not* peculiar to ego uses, but is, rather, characteristic of a much more inclusive range of discourse.

First, the claims made in the parenthetical-verb analysis of ego statements also hold for the corresponding non-ego statements. In any use of parenthetical phrases, then, both ego and non-ego uses, there are two kinds of response available. One of these addresses the truth of the belief, etc. The other addresses the question of whether the putative believer *does* have that belief, etc.

To see this more clearly in the case of non-ego uses, consider the following: A says 'B believes that s.' Someone (e.g., C) may respond, addressing the truth of the belief, 'Oh, s isn't the case at all.' Or, someone (e.g., D) may respond, addressing the question of whether B has that belief, 'Oh, B doesn't believe that s anymore.'

Furthermore, the possibility of these two kinds of response has parallels in (at least some) statements not involving parenthetical phrases at all. Parallel to the above comments, we have: A says 'I (or: B and C) like her looks.' One may answer, 'She isn't at all good-looking.' Or, one may answer, 'Oh, you (or: they) don't like her looks at all.'

Part of our problem, then, is to explain why the *one* type of response is appropriate in some contexts and why the *second* is appropriate in some. We will concentrate on the case of belief claims, and will leave implicit the application of our comments to the other cases mentioned.

In what follows, I will talk of B-stating in those cases in which there are relevant comments addressed to whether the individual contextually indicated has the belief in question, and of T-stating in those cases in which there are relevant comments addressed to whether the belief is true or not. (These two categories are not mutually exclusive.)

I can now state that I take the concern of this chapter to be the elucidation, within the framework introduced in the opening chapters (as supplemented in this chapter), of two phenomena brought into focus by our consideration of parenthetical verb writings referred to. The first of these two phenomena is that there is a parenthetical use of the verb 'to believe', i.e., that 'I believe that s.' can be uttered in certain contexts so that one will thereby be indicating that he is somewhat confident that s.

The second of these is that some instances of uttering 'I believe that s.' are instances of T-stating, i.e., are instances in which there are *relevant* comments addressed to whether or not s.

Before attempting to address these two phenomena directly I would like to make some brief comments in the philosophy of communication.[4] After this I will return to address the concern of this chapter itself.

The observation of some phenomenon may provide the observer with certain information[5] which he did not have before that observation. Thus, one may look at a glass of beer and see that the beer does not have a foamy head. This may be a case of learning that the beer has lost its head. Similarly, one may hear a splashing noise coming from the bathroom and learn that someone is taking a bath.

In what follows, I will focus attention on phenomena under a description, that is, phenomena which are understood as being correctly described in some explicit way. I will call a phenomenon seen under a description a D-phenomenon. Thus, one phenomenon (simpliciter) amounts to an indefinitely large number of D-phenomena.

Then, coming to accept that a phenomenon is an instance of some D-phenomenon provides one with certain information.

---

[4]For a more extensive formulation of some of the ideas to be presented immediately below, see my "On Behavior and Communication," forthcoming in the trans-disciplinary journal *The Human Context*.

[5]I take the notion of information to be noncommittal about its correctness; I do not take 'That was incorrect information.' to be self-contradictory.

Trivially, of course , it provides the one concerned with the information that the given phenomenon is a certain (explicit) D-phenomena.

But this is not all of the information therein provided. Given for instance, that Joe realizes that Burt has just knocked something over, Joe's seeing a damaged teapot on the floor may also bring him to the (correct) belief that Burt has just broken the teapot (in the way in which beliefs may be generated as sketched in the preceding chapter).

Stated more generally, an individual may come to a given phenomenon with accepted beliefs. We can in what follows refer to these collectively as his background assumptions. Then, there will be certain bits of information accepted by the individual on his having taken something to be a certain D-phenomenon. Taking the background assumptions as A_b, and the claim that the given phenomenon is a certain D-phenomenon as D_p, then there is a set of statements S_{ad} derivable from A_b and D_p together, but not from A_b alone. (See below for comments on this notion of derivability.) Such a set is the set of information conveyed (to a particular individual) by a phenomenon's being a particular D-phenomenon. A message of the D-phenomenon is any member of this set.

And if S_p is the set of all statements derivable from A_b and from all of the D_p (that the phenomenon is a D1-phenomenon, a D2-, a D3-, . . . , and a Dn-phenomenon) accepted by the individual, S_p is what is communicated to that individual by that phenomenon. (The inclusiveness of the notion of a phenomenon is to allow for the inclusion as phenomena (or as D-phenomena) of happenings, occurrences, actions, behavior, states, etc.)

This notion of the communication of points of information is independent of questions about the intentions of particular individuals. If Pat blushes (in spite of herself), another may thereby come to know that Pat is embarrassed. But this is so regardless of what Pat's intentions about letting others know of her embarrassment. Similarly one may unintentionally slip on a runner (a kind of rug, not a person) and thereby (unintentionally) inform others that he is an oaf. (Cf. Gogol's madman.)

Concerning the notion of derivability introduced above, I have considered three alternative analyses, each with its advantages. The basic analysis is the following: X is derivable assuming Y if and only if Y provides reasonable grounds for accepting X. What is to count as Y's being reasonable grounds for X can be taken as:

(1) X can be deduced from Y,

(2) Y provides conclusive (non-entailing) grounds for X, or,

(3) Y provides some (but not conclusive) grounds for X.

I have come to the opinion that (3) most closely mirrors our intuitive notion. As a short example: Holding that Bill's yawn shows that Bill is bored is an instance in which one employs the weakest, i.e., the third, notion of one claim's being derivable from another. (Whether or not such instances of gleaning information from what one notices amount to cases of jumping to irrational conclusions or of being insightful seems to rely at least in part on extra-logical considerations (even taking evidence relations as a kind of logical consideration), e.g., on whether such information is correct.)

Note furthermore that this notion of communication is one which easily allows not only for verbal communication (e.g., communicating that s by saying that s) but also for nonverbal communication, and for communicating not only by certain behavior or actions (by saying something, by shaking one's head, by yawning, by staring into space, etc.), but by means other than actional (by having clammy hands, by having a flushed face, by having lipstick on one's collar, etc.). We have allowed for this wide range by having explicated the notion of communicating something (information) in terms of the similarly wide notion of D-phenomena.

With this sketch at our disposal I think that we can now return to the concern of this chapter. I will first try to account for the parenthetical use of 'believe' and then for T-stating. (See above for a more precise statement of these two.)

How is it, then, that one can utter 'I believe that s.' in some contexts and thereby communicate to his listeners that he is (only) somewhat confident that s? We can now restate this issue in terms just introduced. What I want to explain is how there can be a parenthetical use of 'believe' without assuming an ambiguity, etc. in the word 'believe'. Restated, how can one by uttering 'I believe that s.' in certain contexts, communicate that he is somewhat confident that s in such a way that the 'I believe' is that which communicates the degree of confidence?

Part of what I have to say on the question is made more difficult and perhaps even obscured by the fact the system of transcription presently used for English uses only very rough indications of the stress and of intonation patterns of the spoken language. (We have italics, exclamation and question marks, and a paucity of other means.) With this made explicit, let me continue.

The status of a given phenomenon is a function of the range of phenomena which might have obtained in the given context. A particular instance of this is seeing one's doing something as one action out of a certain range (of actions). And a particular instance of this latter is seeing one's saying something as one statement out of a certain range (of statements). I called upon this in addressing Paul's statement in front of the portrait in the museum. (See my final comments in the second chapter on the "in *these* days" part of what Paul said.)

In the present context, an utterance of 'I believe that s.' can be seen as contrastable with utterances of 'I believe that s.', 'I doubt that s.', etc. Given the fact that the speaker had the option of saying any one of these, we can understand his saying "I believe that s." as a manifestation of his wanting to utter this sequence rather than any of the others. We might take this utterance, then, as grounds for attributing this desire to him, and take this desire as grounds for holding that he is only somewhat confident that s. In this way, certain utterances of 'I believe that s.' may be parenthetical uses.

The preceding, of course, presupposes that each instance of the written 'I believe' is read with a particular intonation. I know of no precise way of indicating this intonation pattern, but I can describe it as one in which the syllable 'lieve' (of 'believe') is pronounced either with a rising and then falling pitch or at a pitch markedly higher than that of the preceding syllable. (Somewhat inadequately describable as with a hesitating *tone* of voice.)

That is, we might more adequately distinguish not only 'I believe that s.' from 'I know that s.', etc., but also 'I believe that s.' as a transcription of the sequence with a "hesitating" (cf. above) intonation pattern from the same written sentence as a transcription of the same sequence with a "confident" pattern; e.g., one in which each syllable of 'I believe' is of approximately the same stress, duration, and pitch as each other (with slight major stress on 'lieve'). In a more thorough presentation it might also be necessary to indicate the intonation and stress patterns of 's'; whether "confident", or "questioning", etc.

Given these qualifications, it becomes obvious that with a certain intonation and stress pattern one can communicate total confidence in s by uttering 'I believe that s.' Rather than multiplying the senses of 'believe' to account for what might be an infinity of uses of 'I believe' (one for each of an infinity of degrees of confidence), it seems much more acceptable to take the degree of confidence as communicated by the intonation and stress patterns used.

In this way I hold that 'believe' in 'I believe (am certain) that s.' 'I believe (guess) that s.', 'I believe fervently that s.' etc. is unambiguous (having in all cases the meaning sketched in the first chapter in Ta, Tb, etc.), especially that 'I believe fervently that s.' is not self-contradictory, and that the degree of confidence in s expressed by the speaker is a function of the stress and intonation patterns including those involving the phrase 'I believe') and, where applicable, of the adverbial modifiers of the verb 'believe' (such as 'fervently').

Having stated my position on the parenthetical use of the verb 'believe', let me turn to the second issue, viz., the instances of uttering 'I believe that s.' in which there are *relevant* comments addressed to whether or not s (instances of T-stating).

Below I will introduce four factors in terms of which to explain the relevancy of certain comments made in certain contexts; in particular, in response to statements of the form 'I believe that s.' Before that I will consider some resolutions which I find inadequate.

Several solutions to this problem suggest themselves immediately. Their main fault is that they seem to be entirely ad hoc, as well as incorrect. The first of these suggestions is that the word 'believe' is ambiguous and actually has two or more meanings, or, at least, two or more senses. One might then claim that when B-stating, 'believe' is being used in one sense; when T-stating, it is being used in the second. But it does not seem to be the case that 'believe' has two meanings as has 'division' (army unit, mathematical procedure), nor even two senses as has 'brother' (male sibling, very considerate friend). In order to establish this intuition we would have to enter semantic theory in philosophy of language, but that is beyond the scope of this work. (I rest on the maxim 'Don't multiply senses beyond necessity!')

The second suggestion is that the word 'believe' is being used literally *only* when one is B-stating. But in this case, it is quite difficult to determine which nonliteral use we are employing in the other situation. It is not, *for example*, either that of metaphor (e.g., 'I saw a lion in the cloud.' for 'I saw a cloud in the shape of a lion.') or that of sarcasm (e.g., 'That's a brilliant remark.' for 'That's an inane remark.') Again, a justification of this intuition (which will not be given here) would require a sojourn in philosophy of language.

Perhaps we might clarify this problem by analyzing a similar case. The one I have in mind is that concerning the statement 'I'm sorry for having done that.' We might say that the parallel here would be in taking this statement in some contexts as a report (viz., that the speaker is sorry) and in others as an apology (viz., for what the speaker is sorry about). Then, there will be contexts in which it will be appropriate to reply to this with 'Oh, you're not sorry at all.', and others with 'Oh don't apologize. It's nothing.' As in the central concern here (with 'I believe that . . .'), we might give as a putative solution to the problem of explaining this duality the claim that 'sorry' is ambiguous or that it is not being used literally in both cases. (Also rejected here.)

What I wish to propose is that in some situations S, it will *become* appropriate to comment, *if* one says 'I'm sorry for having done that.', that (a) 'You ought to be.', (b) 'For doing *what?*', (c) 'I'm surprised that you even would have *thought* of doing that, under *any* conditions.', and (d) 'Oh, you're not sorry at all.' And in some other situations S', it will become appropriate (again, if someone says that he's sorry . . .) to give as comment (e) 'Well, I accept your apology.', and (f) 'At least you're man enough to own up to your errors.', but not (d). But what makes the one set of comments appropriate in the one case and the second set in the other is *not* that the sentence 'I'm sorry for having done that.' means something different in the two cases, but rather that *the circumstances effect what comments will be relevant, appropriate.*

A short example might make this last point somewhat clearer. In saying 'Bartok was a great composer.' you may be agreeing with what has just been said (e.g., if this was that Bartok was great) or you may be disagreeing. And of course in one it will then be appropriate to say 'Ah, you agree!' and in the other 'I still must disagree with you.' But it is in virtue of the fact that your sentence *means* the same thing in both cases that you *use* it in one to agree and in the other to disagree. (That meaning *is* use is less than obviously true, at least in any straightforward way). What differs here is *not* what the sentence means, but the situation in which it is uttered. (Cf. sarcasm.) And it is in virtue of the difference in circumstances that makes some comments relevant (e.g., 'Yes, that's just what I just said.') and others irrelevant (e.g., 'You mustn't know contemporary music too well if you say that.').

If this general claim is applied to the problem we're trying to understand, it will prove to be enlightening only if it can explain how comments are or are not relevant in terms of the differences in attending circumstances, and do so while assuming that 'I believe' has the same meaning in all cases, viz., the meaning delineated sketchily in our opening chapters. (Cf. Ta, etc. above.)

What, then, about a situation determines whether it is appropriate to comment either on (1) the claim believed (the s in 'He believes that s.'), or on (2) whether the person in question *does* hold the belief attributed to him?

In order to answer this, I will now introduce the four relevancy factors mentioned above. The four are the following: (1) the present topic of discussion, (2) the present interests of the group, (3) the statements being questioned at the time, if any, and (4) the questions being asked at the time, if any, etc. This is, of course, not an exhaustive list of relevant factors, but it will be adequate for our purpose here, which is to show how attending circumstances help determine which comments are relevant to conversations.

I will call upon these factors below in discussing four cases which will illustrate the general principle that *which* replies to instances of a given comment (-type) are relevant is a function of the circumstances in which the given comment (-instance) is made.

This discussion will be limited in two ways. First, it will not attempt to explain why *any* reply might be made to a given comment. (One might reply to the comment that it's an envigorating day with "The time which an ant requires to crawl two miles is greater than the halflife of Einsteinium."; not all replies are relevant.)

Second, it will not attempt to provide a *systematic* consideration of what might be called relevancy criteria (criteria for whether a given statement is relevant in a given situation or context). It will, rather, attempt only to illustrate the above-mentioned general principle and to show, in particular, how it is in some contexts appropriate to counter 'I believe that s.' with comments addressed to whether or not s, i.e., how instances of this sentence can be used to T-state.

Case 1. A says that B believes that C lied to him (B) about last week (B11). D's reply is that everything that C said to B was true. We might explain why this reply is relevant in the following way. In saying that B believes B11, A *suggests* (communicates) but does not imply (in the logicians' technical sense) that certain explanations of B's behavior, etc. would be correct, and that B can be expected to act in certain ways in certain circumstances.

Were D's interest in determining which explanation of B's behavior, etc. is most accurate, we would find it relevant for D to talk about whether B does or does not believe B11. But here D's interest is in altering (in other circumstances it might be in insuring that they do *not* change) which actions, etc., will be performed by B. Thus, here D might want B to have confidence in C, not to be angry at or distrustful of C, etc., etc. If D thinks that he can either directly (if D is talking with B) or indirectly (if D is talking to someone who will then try to convince B of D's claim) have B alter his set of beliefs about C (presently including, e.g., B11), then D will find it relevant to talk about whether or not it is true that C lied to B about last week. And in this context we can imagine that by making the comment that he does, D supposes that he will influence B's beliefs in one of the above-mentioned ways, and thereby, B's behavior. And this is why D addresses the question of whether B's belief is true.

This first case exemplifies the fact that in some contexts it is appropriate to address the question of whether the belief in question is true rather than to address that of whether the individual specified has that belief. We explain this by citing the fact that D's interest is not in determining whether in fact B does have the belief which A ascribed to him. (D assumes that B does in fact have it.) It is, rather, in bringing it about that B no longer act as he would were he to have this belief. D hopes to provide B with reasons because of which B might change his relevant beliefs.

In this way, D would have his interests satisfied. We have explained, that is, the relevance of certain comments in terms of the second factor listed above, viz., that of the present interests of the group (of D).

Case 2.   A asks B whether the weather is usually moderate in Ankara during the summer. B answers that he (B) believes that it is (B12). C responds to B's answer by saying that Ankara is usually extremely hot in the summer.

C does not address himself to the question of whether B does in fact have the belief in question, but rather to the question of whether B12 is true. We can explain this by showing that these three are now concerned with the question of what the summer weather in Ankara is like, and especially, that C holds B's answer relevant to that concern. Since this is so, C addresses the question of whether the belief is true.

This second case exemplifies the same fact as the first. We explain this in this case by citing the fact that the group is now answering the question of whether the weather is usually moderate in Ankara during the summer. Since this is the concern of the group, the discussion addresses the question of whether B's belief B12 is true, and not that of whether B holds that belief. This provides, that is, an explanation in terms of the fourth factor listed above, viz., that of the questions being asked at the time.

Case 3.   C, a traveler, stops in a town and asks if he can cross over a given bridge. He mentions that he fears that it might be washed out because of the recent flood in the area. A says that he (A) believes that the old bridge up ahead *is* washed out (B13). B's reply is that it *was* (it *was* washed out), but that the river has subsided and the bridge has been repaired. Here the reply is, of course, for the sake of the third party, C.

Here, as in the first case, were B interested in explaining A's behavior, etc., it would be relevant for him to talk about whether or not A does in fact believe B13. But here the topic of discussion is whether the bridge is (still) washed out. (C's plans depend on whether it is.) In order to allow him (C) to make the most reasonable decision as to how to cross the river, B attempts to determine whether he (C) *can* cross by the bridge. Thus, he talks about the belief (that the bridge is washed out) and not about whether A believes what he says he does.

We explain, that is, the relevance of A's comment in terms of the first factor listed above, viz., that of the present topic of discussion.

This explains why we find it relevant to talk about the bridge and not about A. But, it might be asked: If A is stating a belief, how is this relevant to C's travel plans? We can explain this in the following way: In saying 'I believe that the bridge is washed out.', what A means is just that; he is not speaking ambiguously, metaphorically, etc. But we must remember that it is conceptually appropriate to ask why someone believes something to be the case. That is, people can be asked (with conceptual appropriateness) to justify their beliefs, to state the evidence on which they ground their beliefs, to give reasons which might suggest that their beliefs are reasonable ones, etc. Doing so may be socially inappropriate, but this is *not* the inappropriateness of asking someone why he knows something to be the case (cf. asking someone why he bothered learning some obscure fact), of asking someone if his tallest green idea is sleeping slowly, etc.

Not only is this question conceptually appropriate, but it is also generally supposed (with reason) that one can provide an answer to this question. *Were* this general supposition abandoned, then telling a stranger that you believed that the bridge up ahead was washed out would no longer be of any help to him in deciding which road to take, for he would no longer suppose that you had any reason at all in support of your claim! And *if* so, then *your* claim would give him *no reason whatsoever* for believing that the bridge was out!

Now, it is in this way that in saying that you believe that the bridge is washed out that you are suggesting, i.e., communicating, (not implying in the logician's sense) that you have certain reasons for believing that the bridge is washed out. And it is for this reason that the statement 'I believe that s.' can be relevant to a discussion about whether or not s, and not only to one about the speaker's beliefs. But that this is so does *not* entail that A is speaking nonliterally in this case: 'I believe that.' means here, as elsewhere, 'I believe that.'

Case 4.   A states 'I believe that all men are equal.' B replies that he (A) does *not* believe that all men are equal. Here what B holds to be relevant is how A is to act and perhaps also how he has acted. Perhaps B wants to show A that he (A) has been deceiving himself and that if A wants everyone to treat all others as equals, he ought to make a more conscious effort at acting that way himself. Here, bringing A to realize that he has been deceiving himself might result in his acting in a different manner.

This fourth case exemplifies the fact that in some contexts it is appropriate to address the question of whether the individual specified has the belief attributed to him, rather than to address the question of whether that belief is true. We explain this by citing the fact that B is interested in having A behave in a different way from the way in which he (A) has been behaving. (B believes that he can do this by addressing the question of whether A does believe that all men are equal.)

We have, that is, explained the relevance of B's comment in terms of the second factor listed above, viz., that of the present interests of the group.

The previous discussion together with these four cases show, I think, both that belief claims can be used parenthetically (and yet literally), and also that they can be used to T-state, and that this can all be explained (e.g., in terms of different circumstances, interests, etc.) other than by ad hoc multiplication of senses. This, then, completes the task of this chapter.

Chapter IV

MIND-POSSESSORS AND ROBOTS

We can now address ourselves to a problem which has already arisen in our discussion, but which we have not yet handled systematically. There are cases in which it is not obvious either that the individual in question is an MP or that the individual in question is not an MP. These borderline cases have been a topic of discussion in the philosophy of mind for several centuries.

To take just one example, Descartes claimed that the "lower" animals ("brutes") have no minds, that they are only animated machines.[1] Gassendi argued in reply to Descartes' writing that animals do, in fact, possess minds.[2]

We might consider the controversy about *this* borderline case. But rather than that, let us turn to another problematic case, that of robots (primarily because of the more recent interest and discussion of this latter case). I will take as a workable characterization of robots one such as that presented by Ziff:

> I want the right sort of robots. They must be automata and without doubt machines.
>
> I shall assume that they are essentially computing machines, having microelements and whatever micro-

---

[1] E.g., *Discourse on Method*, trans. L. J. Lafleur (New York, The Liberal Arts Press, Inc., 1956), Part V, where Descartes refuses to attribute to animals any of those functions "which are dependent on thinking and which belong to us as men." (p. 30).

[2] E.g., Gassendi's objections to the *Meditations* in "Objections V, Relative to Meditations II," Sect. 7, esp. pp. 145f., of *Philosophical Works of Descartes*, II, trans. E. S. Haldane and G. R. T. Ross (New York, Dover Publications, Inc. 1955), where Gassendi argues for the position that brutes have free will, reason, etc. Cf. Spinoza, *Ethics* (New York, Hafner Publishing Co., 1960), Part IV, Prop. XXXVII, Note 1, p. 215.

mechanisms may be necessary for the functioning of
these engineering wonders. . . .

And if it is clear that our robots are without doubt
machines then in all other respects they may be as
much like men as you like. They may be the size of men.
When clothed and masked they may be virtually in-
distinguishable from men in practically all respects:
in appearance, in movement, in the utterances they
utter, etc. . . .

But unmasked the robots are to be seen in all their
metallic lustre. What is in question here is not whether
we can blur the line between a man and a machine and
so attribute feelings to the machine. The question is
whether we can attribute feelings to the machine and
so blur the line between a man and a machine.[3]

Can, then, robots (machines, computers) think? Can they
have wants? beliefs? intentions? Can they feel pain? perceive?
That is, are they the kind of things that can do, have, feel these?
Do they, in short, have minds? Are they MPs?

These questions are of philosophical importance insofar as
they illuminate certain traditional problems concerning the
status of mental concepts. Philosophers suppose, and hope,
that (adequate) answers to these questions will also propose
analyses justifying or substantiating them. These analyses will,
supposedly, make it more obvious what grounds we have for
attributing mental properties in specific cases, what presuppositions we make in these cases by which we differentiate
these from other cases, whether these grounds are purely
behavioral, etc., etc. It will be the purpose of this chapter to
sketch such aspects of the "logic" of mental concepts.

If we turn to the answers given to these questions by
philosophers, we find, for example (to consider just three
thinkers for the moment), Wittgenstein suggesting at several
places that the questions themselves are somewhat odd, that
the answer is that machines obviously cannot (a conceptual

---

[3]"The Feelings of Robots," *Analysis*, vol. 19, No. 3 (1959), Sect. 1.

impossibility) think, etc. In *The Blue Book* we find, for example, "The trouble is rather that the sentence, "A machine thinks (perceives, wishes)": seems somehow nonsensical."[4] He makes a similar but somewhat more sophisticated point in his *Remarks on the Foundations of Mathematics*.[5]

In sharp contrast with this are the claims of A.M. Turing, who gladly talks of machines acting deliberately, (not) attempting to act in certain ways, etc.: "The machine (programmed for playing the game) would not attempt to give the *right* answers to the arithmetic problems. It would deliberately introduce mistakes in a manner calculated to confuse the interrogator."[6]

J. von Neumann makes similar assumptions in his *The Computer and the Brain*: "A code . . . must contain, in terms that the machine will *understand* and *purposively obey*, instructions . . . that will cause the machine to *examine* every order it gets and *determine* whether this order has the structure appropriate to an order of the second machine."[7]

In this chapter I will address the thesis that robots, etc., cannot have beliefs, wants, thoughts, intentions, etc. This thesis will be referred to as "T".

The bulk of the chapter will be divided into three parts. In the first, I will review some of the more common arguments given in *support* of T, and show why they are either inadequate or confused (or both). In the second part, I will make explicit what I take to be the underlying issues in terms of which one might satisfactorily determine the ultimate acceptability or unacceptability of T. This will amount to a suggestion that one refocus attention from such problems as raised in part one of

---

[4]*The Blue and The Brown Books* (New York, Harper Books, 1965), p. 47. Cf. p. 16, and *Philosophical Investigations, op. cit.*, Part I, Section 360.

[5]*Remarks on the Foundations of Mathematics*, trans. G. E. M. Anscombe (London, The Macmillan Co., 1956), part IV, Sections 1-4.

[6]"Computing Machinery and Intelligence," *Mind*, vol. 59 (1950), p. 448, parentheses and emphasis his.

[7]*The Computer and the Brain* (New Haven, Yale University Press, 1963), p. 72, my emphases.

this chapter to those addressed in the following chapter. Thus, part two will be a preliminary to an evaluation of T. In the third, which may be considered as a brief addendum to the other parts of this chapter, I will show what has led some philosophers and psychologists to take other positions regarding, for example, the questions (a) Do robots think, etc?, and (b) Are what we take to be human beings really MPs? (e.g., certain Skinnerians).

I

Let us turn, to some arguments presented in support of T. The examples I present have appeared in recent literature, either as (a) arguments presented as (partial) justification of the thesis T in articles arguing for T, or as (b) arguments presented and then attacked in articles arguing against T. We will consider each in order, and show why the argument in question is unacceptable. (For some arguments which I will not discuss, see some of the (straw-men) positions advanced by Turing, *op. cit.*)

(1) If something is programmed to do x, then in being completely controlled by its programming, it does not "really" do x, it just acts as if it were doing x.

If, however, a robot is programmed to write out the answer 'four' when the input is the question 'What is the sum of two plus two?', and nothing goes wrong (the power supply is not cut off, the robot does not explode, (in older models) no tubes below, etc., etc.), then the robot *does* write out this answer ("really!!"). Gunderson, for example, points out this non sequitur in his "Cybernetics and Mind-Body Problems."[8] It is interesting to note that when he claims that some given robot must be a conscious being since it is "programmed to think certain

---

[8]"Cybernetics and Mind-Body Problems," U.C.L.A., Los Angeles, 1965, mimeograph. For an abstract of this article, see *The Journal of Philosophy*, vol. 62, No. 21 (No. 4, 1965), p. 657.

things, feel certain ways, and so on,"[9] Gunderson is, of course, begging the question: What is to be asked here is whether or not a robot *can* be programmed to think, etc.

That is, this typical argument *for* T allows much too much when it accepts that a robot can be programmed to think, believe, etc.

(2) It is odd to say 'The robot is conscious.'[10] Therefore, it makes no sense to talk of ascribing consciousness to robots.

The importance of oddity of utterances in *suggesting* further conceptual analysis is not being denied. But oddity *merely* suggests investigation: if anything of philosophical importance is to be established, what must be shown is *why* the utterance in question is odd. It might be odd for any number of reasons, one of which might be merely that we never realized that robots are conscious.

But the observations of the preceding paragraph can also be applied in response to certain arguments *against* T made on such linguistic grounds. Gunderson notes that "it is no longer linguistically vagrant or odd to say "A machine composed this music" or "This machine makes better chess openings than I do" and so forth."[11] Even if these utterances ars *not* balked at in present-day English, we still have to explain *why* not. For it *might* be merely that people hold this to be either a non-literal use of 'composed', etc., or, at least, an extended use; people might still claim that robots can't "really" compose, etc.

(3) We can predict the behavior of computers, robots, etc., but not that of human beings. Therefore the former do not have minds of their own, do not have thoughts, beliefs, wants, etc., while the latter do.

This can be attacked on two grounds, one for each of the two conjuncts in the premiss. Scriven argues that the addition

---

[9]"Interview with a Robot," *Analysis*, vol. 23 (1963), p. 139.

[10]Paul Ziff, "The Feelings of Robots," *op. cit.*, Sect. 3.

[11]"Interview with a Robot," *op. cit.*, p. 138. Cf. Section 5 of Putnam's "Minds and Machines," pp. 138-164 of S. Hook, ed., *Dimensions of Mind* (New York, Collier Books, 1961).

of a quantum randomiser to a computer would make, even "in principle," unpredictable what the output will be, at least according to contemporary physicists.[12]

On the other hand, we might claim that there is no theoretic reason to suppose that such prediction might not someday be available. But we can (and I would want to) claim this (as well) for the prediction of human behavior. No argument which proves that human behavior cannot be modelled in a nomological framework has to my knowledge ever been adequately proposed.

And since it is likely that the level of complexity of computer output might some day be comparable to that of human behavior, it seems probable that in future ages it will be as simple (or complicated) to explain the one as the other. But: See the second part of this chapter for further related comments.

(4) In order to construct a machine capable of performing on the level of complexity of a human brain, we would have to employ organic tissue. But then we would not have a machine at all.

Scriven argues that we could synthesize organic tissue and that we might then still have a machine.[13] But this argument and counter-argument both confuse the question of whether robots, etc., might think, etc., with that of whether or not we might one day synthesize life in a laboratory (factory?). What we are addressing here is *not* the question of whether one will ever be able technologically to create a synthetic living being, but rather the question of whether there will ever be anything which is obviously a robot to which we will ever correctly attribute thoughts, beliefs, etc. Leaving the first question open, one accepting T is committed to answering the latter negatively. For an elaboration of the above-mentioned distinction, see Ziff, "The Feelings of Robots," *op. cit.*, Section 1, and for a criticism of Scriven's point, see Watanabe, "Comments on Key Issues."[14]

---

[12]"Thet Compleat Robot: A prolegomena to Andriodology," Sect. 5, p. 119, in S. Hook, ed., *Dimensions of Mind, op. cit.*

[13]*Ibid.*, p. 115.

[14]P. 136, especially part of the section entitled "Comments on Professor Scriven's Presentation," in S. Hook, ed., *Dimensions of Mind, op. cit.*

(5) A robot will never respond to us in the same way that other human beings do. Therefore, we assert on the basis of this difference that robots are mindless but that human beings have minds.[15]

This argument is rather weak for several reasons. First of all, there is no a priori reason to hold that advancements in technology will not some day allow engineers to design robots which can simulate human behavior perfectly. (Hook, I suppose, would *not* be happy to say here that nonetheless human beings respond humanly and robots robotly.) But, moreover, even if the premiss of this fifth argument is true, it is invalid to conclude from it that robots have no minds. For even dogs respond differently to us than do people, but we have no qualms whatsoever in attributing a mind to dogs. Until it is explicated just how the responses differ, the claim has no weight.

(6) The central nervous system is not a discrete state machine. But a digital computer is (one sort of) a discrete state machine.[16] Turing, in arguing against T, stipulates that this information is unavailable to the players in his "imitation game."

Briefly, the "imitation game" is a game played by a computer and two people. The computer and one of the two people answer questions asked them by the second person. The computer "attempts" to "deceive" the interrogator into believing that it is the person and that the person is the robot. The person answering the questions tries to convince the interrogator that he/she is human and that the other contestant is the robot. The answers given by the two contestants provide the interrogator with the *sole* information on the basis of which he must decide which is the human and which is the robot. Turing asks whether, in playing this game, the robot will be more successful at "deceit" than would a person replacing it. Turing continues, declaring that the above information about the structure of the central nervous system cannot be used to argue for

---

[15]E.g., S. Hook, "A Pragmatic Note," p. 185 in S. Hook, ed., *Dimensions of Mind, op cit.*

[16]Turing, *op. cit.*, esp. section 7.

T. He does this by building this limitation into the rules of his "game." We are not, however, limited to the condition built into Turing's imitation game that one deciding whether or not some X is a robot can base that decision only on the answers to questions posed to it.

We are, then, free to make use of the information given in the premiss of the sixth argument. Even if we accept this premiss (as true), however, we cannot thereby establish the thesis T. For at most the premiss establishes that a digital computer is not the best *model* for a human's central nervous system. That, however, is irrelevant to our present question, for we are not at all asking if these computers model our brain but rather whether they think, etc. And two things may have radically different structures and still be able to perform the same tasks. Recall how differently washing machines are built from washer-women, yet both can wash clothes. (This example is taken from Gunderson.[17])

(7) I can (psychological possibility) have attitudes towards other people that I can not have towards machines. Paul Weiss, for example, writes "Should we find a machine which we can love, we *must* say of it that it has human nature and human powers. We *will*, in short, divide beings, all of whom behave in the same way, into two classes, calling "men" those which are in principle within our powers to love, and calling "machines" those which we cannot possibly love."[18]

Aside from the prima facie implausible consequence that we should call dogs and beloved pets "men" (Insofar as they and humans both sneeze, etc., they *do* behave in the same way. And many people do love dogs.), this argument has a more central weakness. For whether or not we are psychologically capable of loving some x depends on us, on our beliefs about x, etc. But these are not properties of *x*, but rather of *us*. An adequate justification of this last point would require a brief metaphysical analysis of properties, but here I can just add

---

[17]"Cybernetics and Mind-Body Problems," *op. cit.*, p. 2.
[18]"Love in a Machine Age," p. 179, my emphases, in S. Hook, ed., *Dimensions of Mind, op. cit.*

that, intuitively, if my friend Bob suddenly falls in love with a computer, what has changed (for the worse) is Bob, and not the computer.

Although what Weiss says is not at all plausible, it *is* true that the beliefs that we have about computers do affect what we are willing to say about them. This will be further explicated in part two.

(8) Machines cannot reproduce. Therefore they are not alive, and therefore they have no minds.

First of all, there *are* self-copying machines. If this is not to count as reproduction, it is because machines are held *not* to be the sort of thing which can be alive. But this is irrelevant the question at hand. It addresses itself rather to the question of whether we have designed a synthetic living organism on the drawing board.[19]

Secondly, of course, it does not follow that simply because something cannot reproduce that it is not alive. Consider sterile members of the human race, and all mules.

The above is just a sampling of inadequate justifications for T. Rather than continuing with this negative criticism, especially since the other arguments are much *less* plausible than the eight already given, I would like to turn now to the more positive part of this chapter.

II

Some have held that all we ever observe of others (things which we assume to be other people) is behavior of a certain sort—for example, someone moving out of the way of some falling object. And that it is simply on the basis of such behavior that we attribute certain mental properties to some person—for example, his being *afraid of* being hit, or his *believing* that moving will keep him from being hit by the

---

[19]Cf. the Watanabe criticism of Scriven, *loc. cit.*

falling object. Some continue that what we mean when we
say that someone has a certain mental property is that he has
a disposition to behave in a certain way. Recall that for Ryle,
e.g., both 'know' and 'believe' are dispositional verbs of this
sort.[20]

If this is so, then it follows that were machines to (have
the dispositions to) behave in these same ways, we should
also say that they know, believe, etc. Note, as an aside, that
the fact that we consider the perfect copying of (human)
behavior by a robot *not* to be adequate reason for claiming that
the robot is an MP is (of itself inconclusive) evidence against
the preceding behaviorist claim.

A similar claim which, however, is not committed to behaviorism, is that of Gunderson, in his "Cybernetics and Mind-
Body Problems", *op. cit.* There he distinguishes between "low-
powered" psychological phrases, such as 'follows rules', 'solves
problems', 'checks results', and 'corrects mistakes', and "high-
powered" psychological terms, such as 'thinks', 'believes', 'understands', and 'knows'. Gunderson assumes that the low-powered
phrases enter into ascriptions made to a machine on the basis of a
process or result (or both) brought about by a stimulus (which,
I suppose, is some input) or what Gunderson calls S-ascrip-
tions.[21] He then argues that since in the case of humans, "we
often argue for a given high-powered term being applicable
on the basis of certain low-powered terms being applicable",
we must explain why we accept the applicability of the same
low-powered terms to machines (in some given case), while
nonetheless disallowing the application to them of the high-
powered term in question.[22]

Although I will return to Gunderson's claim that the low-
powered ascriptions can be made to machines with no change
in sense, I will still try to provide such an explanation (as
called for by Gunderson's last claim). We will return to the
question of whether robots do "solve problems", etc., considering

---

[20]*Concept of Mind,, op. cit.*, p. 133.
[21]*Op cit.*, defined on pp. 9f.
[22]*Ibid.*, p. 12.

reasons for holding that we are not speaking literally in such cases, and thus that these low-powered psychological terms are *not* literally ascribable to robots, etc.

Where both the behaviorists and Gunderson go wrong is where they agree. Both argue as if our only grounds for making ascriptions to entities is their *behavior* and that thus, if we can make machines which can behave as human do, we ought to (if we are to be consistent in our use of language?) say that these machines, too, think, etc.

Note in this context the following argument by Michael Simon:

> It makes no sense to say that a thing is acting *as if* it has a certain state of consciousness or feels a certain way unless there is some demonstrably relevant feature that supports the use of "as if" as a qualifying stipulation. And to be unable to specify the way in which mentalistic descriptions apply to objects of equal *behavioral* capacities is to be unable to distinguish between the consciousness of a person and that of an automaton. If we find that we can effectively describe the *behavior* of a thing that performs in the way a human being does only by employing the terminology of mental states and events, then we cannot deny that such an object possesses consciousness.[23]

And, similarly, the following of Margaret Boden's claims:

> We could thus only apply the predicate 'perceives' in its full sense to a machine if the *behavior* of the machine were sufficiently complex, autonomous and flexible for us to speak of voluntary as well as involuntary [nonvoluntary?] activity.[24]

---

[23]"Could There Be A Conscious Automaton?", *American Philosophical Quarterly*, vol. 6, No. 1 (Jan., 1969), p. 78, last two emphases mine.

"[24]Machine Perception," *The Philosophical Quarterly*, vol. 19, No. 74 (Jan., 1969), p. 45, emphasis mine. I do not think that this concluding remark of hers does full justice to her article.

I agree rather strongly with what Gunderson states in his "Imitation Game": "What I instead want to emphasize is that what we would say about Peterson [some human being] in countless other situations is bound to influence what we say about him in the imitation game."[25] But it is essential to realize that we can say more about something (a robot, a man) than that it *behaves* in a certain way. I will argue that the answer to the question of whether robots think, have beliefs, etc., or not, is not at all to be found in the differences between a robot's behavior and a human's, but rather, in the difference between a robot and a human.

This argument, still to be given, will also suggest, I think, why Scriven's first R. George Washington (robot) to say 'Yes.' to the question of whether it has feelings will *not* thereby show that it is a person.[26] Scriven presents his case basically as follows: We *teach* a robot English, then *introduce him to* the *concepts* of truth and falsity, and then make it necessary that the robot *tell the truth* by adding a circuit to it which renders *lying* impossible.[27] Scriven then answers the "objections that we cannot be sure it understands the questions" by commenting that "it seems to me that we can reply that we have every good reason for thinking that it does understand, as we have for thinking this of other *people*."[28]

As I have just asserted above (to be supported below), there are relevant considerations to be addressed prior to concluding that Scriven's robot understands. These may well establish that it does *not* understand, and does not understand because robots *cannot* understand, because they *cannot* comprehend, cannot think—are not MPs!! And let me emphasize here that our ground for claiming this would not be limited to the consideration that they *behave* differently from human beings (so do dogs, etc.), even if they do.

If our deliberations ultimately establish the thesis T, then

25"The Imitation Game," *Mind*, vol. 73, N.S. (1964), p. 240.
26See section 12 of his "The Compleat Robot," *op. cit.*, esp. p. 133.
27*Ibid.*, p. 132.
28*Ibid.*, p. 133, his emphasis.

one reason that the robot's 'Yes.' would *not* tell us that he is an MP is that his answer would not be a case of an earnest assertion. For only MPs can be earnest, have intentions, etc. Robots, not being MPs, could not have intentions. Robots could not intend to deceive and so *no* robot would require an extra circuit to render lying impossible. The printing of (a coded punch-card for) the word 'yes' is not always an earnest assertion: Robots just wouldn't be earnest. Nor, of course, would they be deceitful.

Nor could they be *taught* a language, although a language (or perhaps only a "language") could be programmed into (a sufficiently complex type of) them. Nor could we get them to understand the concepts of truth and falsity, since they couldn't understand anything at all. Compare this with Danto's argument that the machine must answer 'No.', since, being a machine it cannot have feelings: "we can readily predict the outcome of the experiment without going to the trouble and expense of building a Scriven machine."[29]

As I have said above, the answer to the question posed at the outset of this chapter is to be found not (only) in determining the differences (if any) between the behavior of robots and that of people, but in the differences (if any) between robots and people. It is time to explicate this claim.

The essential difference between robots and people (essential, that is, to our giving an adequate answer to our question) would be that different systems of explanations would be called upon in the two cases to explain adequately, properly (not misleadingly), simply, etc., etc., the behavior, states, etc., which are observed.

To state this differently: The theory which we think will more insightfully, clearly, heuristically, simply, etc., etc., explain the data at hand (Here: the behavior, *et alia*) will itself *put a limit on which questions* about the behavior (*et alia*) in question *will be* (*conceptually*) *appropriate*. The theoretical framework

---

[29]"On Consciousness in Machines," p. 167, in S. Hook, ed., *Dimensions of Mind, op. cit.*

that we take to fulfill these requirements allows certain explanations and not others. If, that is, one assumes that a given framework Y is not applicable to some kind of entity X, then one must also hold Y-concepts to be inappropriate to a discussion of Xs. In holding that a given concept is inapplicable to Xs, one holds it to be logically or conceptually impossible for an X to exemplify the given concept. (See the Wittgenstein quote and the comment thereupon, directly below.)

In assuming, that is, that a given framework is the most appropriate to use in describing and explaining some phenomenon, one thereby puts a limit on which descriptions and explanations will be allowed and which will not.

A theory, for example, which talks about wants, beliefs, intentions, etc. (includes the words 'want', 'belief', 'intention' as terms in the explanans language) allows for such questions as 'Did he do that because of his intention to please his parents?' One which does *not* talk about these does *not* allow these questions.

And insofar as we take a given framework to be applicable to a given group of entities and phenomena but not to some other group, we allow the possibility of describing the first group in terms of the concepts in questions, but disallow the possibility of describing the second group in these concepts. This, I think, is the point of Wittgenstein's "The limit of the empirical—is *concept formation.*"[30]

In the present case, we can consider two kinds of theoretical framework, which I shall call M-theories and C-theories. An M-theory is a theoretical framework which allows for nomological explanation in terms of such *m*ental concepts as beliefs, wants, etc.[31] A C-theory is one which allows for nomological explanation in terms of such *c*omputer concepts as closed circuits, digital computers, circuit breakdowns, programming, pushdown storage, finite state Markov processes, etc.

---

[30]*Remarks on the Foundations of Mathematics, op. cit.,* Part III, Sect. 29, his emphasis.

[31]Similar to the one sketched above, or to the one outlined in A. Goldman, *Action,* Doctoral thesis, Princeton University, 1965.

We have yet to explain just what is involved in an individual's assuming, for example, that an M-theory is more insightful, less misleading, clearer, simpler, etc., than some other theory. I will not attempt to explicate this notion here, but will limit myself to making comments on the implications of this claim.

First, if what I have claimed above is true, then *one could support T in the following way*: In general the most adequate explanation of human behavior, i.e., of what people do, will be in terms of an M-theory. The output of computers, robots, etc., however, is best explained in terms of the circuits which compose the robot, the tapes which are given to it, the opening of certain circuits because of tubes being blown out (in those older robots, etc., which have tubes), etc., etc. That is, when we want to explain the output of a robot, we look to a C-theory. As long as we *do,* the assumption of the conceptual inapplicability of an M-theory to robots provides us with an immediate answer to the question of whether some robot has some given belief, viz., that it doesn't (since it *can't* have any belief). *What would have to be argued for* if T is to be adequately justified is that some theory other than an M-theory, such as a C-theory, will always be a more illuminating, etc., framework in which to explain a robot's output other than an M-theory would be. (This issue will be addressed in the fifth chapter.)

One implication of my position is that the (conceptual) correctness or incorrectness of attributing mental predicates to something, of claiming that something has or doesn't have beliefs, wants, etc., of claiming that something is or is not an MP, will depend on the assumptions which are in force concerning what will count as an illuminating explanation of some given (human, robot, etc.) behavior. This in turn suggests that further scientific development can make a difference in our acceptance of T only insofar as it leads us to believe that a C-theory is *not* adequate to explain the output of some robot but that some M-theory is.

Each of such factors as that of the future sophistication of robot construction influences the over-all reasonableness of assuming that an M-theory is (in-)applicable to robots. If at any given time, however, it is held that all of the relevant factors are such that it is more reasonable to assume that M-theories are inapplicable to robots than to assume that they are applicable, then it will also be held that robots, etc., are not MPs, and therefore, cannot have beliefs, wants, etc.

But the preceding suggests that one committed to T is also committed to the claim that changes in robot behavior will result in alteration (complication) of some C-theory rather than abandonment of the C-theory which has explained all that it has about robots, suggested ways of making more complicated robots, etc. This too will be addressed in chapter five.

It might be argued that what I am saying commits me to the following: If scientific development is such that all of the behavior of human beings is at some future time adequately and simply explicable without reference to an M-theory, e.g. (N.B.: *not* 'i.e.'), completely in terms of an NC-theory (a theory combining *n*europhysiological and "*c*onventional" explanation; the former adequately explaining all facts of an individual's moving the latter explaining certain of what Goldman has called "higher acts"[32]), then we will no longer find it appropriate to attribute mental properties to people. Or, in other words, that we will no longer have the distinction between MPs and non-MPs, and that it will be the former notion which is assimilated to the latter and not vice versa.

Firstly (since it is a shorter comment), since the implication of my thesis is here held to be a hypothetical, we can say that we never *will* find that any other theory of human action is as illuminating, etc., as is an M-theory, and that, therefore, we will never be led to accept the claim that people (or what we take to be people) do *not* have beliefs, wants, etc.

Secondly, which explanation is considered most adequate, illuminating, etc., depends of course on the context in which the explanation is being offered. What one is willing to say depends upon when and where and to whom he is talking. The

---

[32]*Op. cit.* Similarly, consider Danto's distinction between basic and non-basic actions, e.g., in his "What We Can Do," *Journal of Philosophy*, vol. 60, No. 15 (July 18, 1963), pp. 435-445.

philosopher may believe firmly that he doesn't "really" know anything, yet earnestly tell his little daughter nonetheless that he knows she's been naughty and that he forgives her. The physicist who believes firmly that even a metal slab is not "really" solid, nonetheless complains to the laboratory assistant for bringing him a perforated, sievelike board when what he asked for was a solid sheet and not for what was brought. What is an adequate, illuminating, etc., explanation in one context will be jejune and superficial in another.

One implication of this is that the question of whether theoreticians of human behavior in a formal situation will some day avoid all use of M-theory is independent of whether they as people in an informal context will be willing to say that we are MPs.

One example of this which can now be given is that we are normally (as "men in the street") willing to say that someone (in some context) did x because his emotions took control of him and led him to act in an irrational way. This way of talking presupposes a faculty psychology similar to that proposed by Plato.[33] But simply because we can be made to understand what someone is doing in a rather rough (but in some contexts perfectly adequate) way by this type of explanation, we are in no way thereby committed to arguing for a faculty psychology when discussing schizophrenia with psychiatrists. What we can roughly and adequately understand (for one purpose) by a primitive model in one context need not be what we can understand precisely and adequately (for another purpose) by another, sophisticated model.

It follows that even if we were to hold some day that a (psychiatrically) clinically adequate explanation of certain behavior can only be in terms of an NC-theory, the question of whether or not we were willing to accept explanations (in talking with laymen) in terms of an M-theory is still a completely open one. And this is to say that which theory we hold

---

[33]*Republic*, trans. by Paul Shorey in E. Hamilton and H. Cairns, ed. *Plato: The Collected Dialogues* (New York, Random House, Inc., 1964), Book IV, e.g., 436a-b, 439d.

to provide us with the most illuminating, least misleading, etc., explanation is partially a function of what purposes we have in mind in asking for an explanation, what we assume those we're talking with to know, their interests, etc., etc. And insofar as we hold an M-theory to be (in-)adequate for explaining something's behavior, we will hold the claim 'That thing has beliefs, wants, intentions, etc.', to be conceptually (in)appropriate.

My program of *contrasting* the applicability of an M-theory with that of a C-theory has been suggested to overlook the writings relevant to such a program of such people as Fodor,[34] Putnam,[35] Deutsch,[36] and Miller, Galanter, and Pribram.[37] The general putatively problematic consideration raised in such works is illustrated in the following. Fodor, e.g., writes of a "phase one theory" (which is one that provides the type of psychological explanation which calls upon "hypothetical internal states"[38] to explain observed behavior), holding that it is "compatible with indefinitely many hypotheses about the physiology of the organism."[38] He goes on to claim that "it seems reasonable to maintain that any phase one theory that is compatible with the known facts of neurology must be, *ipso facto,* unacceptable."[39] Somewhat more guardedly, Miller, Galanter, and Pribram hold, "A psychological analysis that can stand up to the neurological evidence is certainly better than one that cannot. The catch, obviously, is in the phrase "stand up to," since considerable prejudice can be involved in its definition."[40]

Such comments as these, then, supposedly bring into doubt

---

[34]Esp. Jerry Fodor, "Explanations in Psychology," pp. 161-179 in M. Black, ed., *Philosophy in America* (Ithaca, Cornell University Press, 1965).

[35]Esp. H. Putnam, "Minds and Machines," *op. cit.*

[36]Esp. J. A. Deutsch, *The Structural Basis of Behavior* (Chicago, University of Chicago Press, 1960).

[37]Esp. G. A. Miller, E. Galanter, K. H. Pribram, *Plans and the Structure of Behavior* (New York, Holt, Rinehart and Winston, Inc., 1960).

[38]Fodor, *op. cit.,* p. 174.

[39]*Ibid.,* p. 176.

[40]Miller, Galanter, and Pribram, *op. cit.,* "Some Neuropsychological Speculations," p. 196.

the basic tack of attempting to determine whether to employ a C-theory or an M-theory because it is possible, *or* least might very well be so, to employ both the one *and* the other, because the two are not (at least obviously) incompatible.

As the preceding discussion should have shown, however— cf. especially the comments on discussions either calling on the notion of a faculty psychology or concerning schizophrenia— there is nothing in what I have said which is committal on the issue of the *general* incompatibility of alternative types of theory (e.g., an M-theory and an NC-theory). My point has been to focus on the issue of explanations *in various contexts.* And the difference in appropriateness between two different types of theory *in various contexts* does not at all require the recognition of a general a priori incompatibility between the two given types. I thus agree with the comment made in this same article (supposedly problematic to the position I am proposing here) of Fodor's:

> of the variety of types of explanation we can give to account for what someone did, the one we want for practical purposes is rarely couched in terms of underlying psychological mechanisms. Analogously, if the insurance agent wants an explanation of the fire, we do not offer him physics. Yet presumably a physical explanation could be given and would be appropriate on certain occasions. Roughly: the appropriateness of an explanation is determined not by the phenomena it seeks to account for but by the question it seeks to answer.[41]

Following this basic line, then, one could justify T if one could establish that an M-theory would be held to be inappropriate to any discussion about robots in any context whatsoever. This is a rather strong claim to establish. I will, however, hold a more extended discussion of this claim until the next chapter.

---

[41]Fodor, *op. cit.,* p. 165.

III

What, then, might we say to explain why certain philosophers have held that machines *can* think? These philosophers, I think, presuppose that certain developments in the construction of computers, robots, etc., will make it more reasonable to explain the computer's (etc.'s) output by use of an M-theory than by use of a C-theory. I can see no possible "knock-down argument" to establish this claim, but I take it that this presupposition is necessary for T. This assumption about the non-applicability of an M-theory to robots will be more fully examined and elaborated in chapter five.

What we have here is a disagreement as to which theoretic framework (which conceptual scheme) is the better one to use in making certain data intelligible. We are still in need, of course, of guidelines for resolving such a disagreement, but I will not attempt to clarify this issue any more than has already been done until the next chapter.

Before that, however, let me apply what has already been said to the illumination of certain rather general claims of recent psychology. This same general point about the presupposition concerning the relative adequacy of different explanatory frameworks sheds light on the obiter dicta of certain psychologists, e.g., certain Skinnerians. Some recent psychologists maintain that all of human behavior will some day be best explained in terms of an SR (stimulus-response) theory. As they hold that this makes no mention of and has no need of supplementation by an M-theory, they claim (programmatically) that we (people) don't "really" have any minds.[42] Although they would not make use of the conceptual-empirical contrast (i.e., they would not talk of the conceptual inappropriateness of talking of human beliefs, wants, etc.), they would, I suppose, argue that such talk is unintelligible, or scientifically

---

[42]The question of whether SR theory *is* independent of M-theory is an open question: see arguments to the contrary in A. Goldman, *op. cit.*, Chapter 5.

unverifiable, or scientifically meaningless, or . . . . I assume by now that we have adequately shown these claims to be false, and will not, therefore, discuss them further.

In closing, we might (as an aside) use this point to make some sense of the claim of Piaget that children use a different conceptual scheme from the one which adults use.[43] If, for example, the child holds it appropriate to talk of the wants and beliefs of a rock in explaining that it fell to earth, rather than to talk of its weight, etc. (The child asks 'Did it want to do that?', comments 'Why, of course, it's heavy. So are you. But why talk of that?', etc.), then we have excellent reason to say that the child *does* have a different conceptual framework from ours; a different set of methodological and theoretic presuppositions about what will be enlightening explanation from ours.

---

[43]E.g., *The Child Conception of the World,* trans. by J. Tomlinson and A. Tomlinson (London, Kegan Paul, Trench, Trubner & Co., Ltd., 1929).

CHAPTER V

THE RANGE OF MENTALISTIC FRAMEWORKS

The position we came to in the preceding chapter is that our answer to the question of whether a given entity (whether a philosopher, a robot, an infant, a dog, or even a rock) has beliefs, wants, emotions, etc., depends on whether or not we can establish that an M-theory (a theory essentially employing mentalistic concepts) can be appropriately used in a given context in reference to that entity. Or, more precisely, establishing that an M-theory can or cannot be appropriately used in *any* given context in discussion about a given entity provides us with a justification for the claim that that entity can or cannot have beliefs, wants, etc. This, of course, is preliminary to our establishing that that entity *has* in fact a certain belief, want, etc.

One could, that is, justify the claim that a robot is not the kind of thing which has beliefs, intentions, wants, emotions, etc., by showing it is in all cases (conceptually) inappropriate to use an M-theory in a discussion about that entity. This inappropriateness is in contrast with the appropriateness of a C-theory, which can (at times) be (conceptually) appropriately used.

This, in turn, could be justified by providing factors in terms of which reasons could be given which provide a basis on which it can be decided whether an M-theory (or, in general: a given conceptual scheme) is (logically) appropriate to a given entity. One could then ground the claim about the inapplicability of an M-theory to robots on the reasons obtained by consideration of these factors. We will refer to these grounding factors as G-factors. It is important to add at this point that the factors we propose should be such that they *clearly* show that M-theory discussions are perfectly appropriate to people and perfectly inappropriate to rocks. I take it that other animals (such as apes, chimpanzees, dogs, cats, rats, etc.) and robots provide us with intermediary cases, and indeed that the question about whether cats or robots have beliefs, etc., arises partially because of just the fact that they are not perfectly clear cases. (Problem cases are essentially problematic.)

In this chapter I will attempt to provide an answer to the question of what factors there are on the basis of which one could justify the claim that a given conceptual scheme is (conceptually) appropriate to some entity. In the application of this answer to the claim that robots are MPs, I will, unfortunately, have to leave some central problems untouched, such as: (1) How much and what kind of a change in a conceptual scheme is required before it is considered to be a new scheme of the same genus as was the scheme before the change was made? That is, what are the grounds for determining that two schemes are not the same scheme but rather two very similar ones? (2) How much and what kind of a change in a conceptual scheme is required before it is considered to be a new scheme of a different genus from the scheme before the change? That is, what are the grounds for determining that two schemes are not the same scheme but rather two different *kinds* of scheme?

A solution to these two problems would be required before one could give a completely adequate evaluation of the claim that robots are MPs. This is so because this solution would be called upon in a justification of the claim that the conceptual scheme resultant from taking a given M-theory (e.g., one used in explaining the behavior, etc. of man) and changing it so as to make it applicable to robots would be neither (1) the same conceptual scheme, nor, (2) a different scheme which was, nonetheless, an M-theory (i.e., an M-theory, but not an M-theory applicable to man).

Because of this, we should consider what follows to be an appendix to the preceding chapter; one that merely presents a preliminary to an adequate evaluation of T, the thesis that robots cannot have beliefs, wants, etc.

Let us focus our attention, then, on the presentation of factors in terms of which one can determine whether a given scheme is applicable to a given entity. In so doing, we can look to the history of philosophy to see if any suggestions pertaining to this problem can be gleaned from the relevant literature.

On one interpretation of Spinoza, for example, he can be seen as discussing the fact that one entity, viz., Deus sive Natura, can be considered as possessing properties which belong to different conceptual schemes (e.g., those belonging to one using mentalistic concepts (his "attributes of thought"), those belonging to one using physicalistic concepts (his "attributes of extension"), etc.) Consider, e.g., the following passage:

> ". . . substance thinking and substance extended are one and the same substance, which is now *comprehended* under this attribute and now under that. . . . [W]hen things are *considered* as modes of thought we must explain the order of the whole Nature or the connection of causes by the attribute of thought alone, and when things are *considered* as modes of extension, the order of the whole of Nature must be explained through the attribute of extension alone, and so with other attributes.[1]

But although Spinoza seems to see that there are situations in which there are alternative conceptual schemes in terms of which to describe, explain, etc., a given phenomenon, a given "slice of reality"; he says almost nothing which might be helpful in deciding which of such schemes is to be used in a given situation.

The analysis which Spinoza proposes in discussing the question of whether it is appropriate to explain God's actions in terms of God's wants, needs, etc., concludes that a certain part of a mentalistic framework cannot be appropriately applied to God.[2] In our parallel problem, we wish to evaluate the

---

[1]*Ethics, op. cit.,* Part II, Proposition VII, Corollary, Note, p. 84, my emphases. Consider also Part I, Prop. XIV, Cor. 1; Part II, Prop. V, VI, and especially Prop. XXI, Note; Part III, Prop. II, Note.

[2]*Ibid.,* Part I, Appendix, pp. 72-78. See also Part I, Prop. XXXIII, Note 2, p. 71; Part IV, Preface, p. 188, etc.

stronger claim that no part of an M-scheme can be appropriately applied to robots.

This interpretation of Spinoza's position suggests the following when we consider it in light of our parallel problem: A given conceptual scheme is applicable to some (kind of) entity or phenomenon only if this application is not responsible for the generation of contradictions. This implies that if (a) a given scheme is applicable to one kind of entity or phenomenon with no contradiction thereby engendered, then if (b) the application of that scheme to some other kind of entity or phenomenon generates contradiction, then (c) one has adequate grounds for claiming that the scheme is inapplicable to this latter kind of entity or phenomenon. We will return to this in a modified form when we introduce specific G-factors, below.

Spinoza, however, did not present a systematic solution to the problem of how to determine which of two competing schemes is or is not appropriate to some given context. This is perhaps because he did not consider it to be a (serious) problem. In any case, we cannot look to Spinoza for more help here, in spite of the fact that he can be taken as providing a general philosophical perspective which ultimately calls for the grounds we are now in search of.

If we look to the philosophy of science for some clues concerning a solution to this problem, we might at first suspect that discussion of the problem of choosing between competing theories would be relevant to our discussion of the problem of choosing between competing conceptual schemes. And this in turn might lead us to the following proposal: Of two competing conceptual schemes, C_1 and C_2, the one which is to be considered more appropriate is the one which provides a simpler explanation of the given phenomenon (or set of phenomena). Note, of course, that we must be able to specify what this phenomenon (this set of phenomena) is in such a way that both of the competing schemes will be logically possible candidates. We must, that is, avoid prejudging this question by a description of the phenomenon which is obviously open to explanation by only one of the two. In general, we would prejudge this question by couching the description in terms which clearly belong to one conceptual scheme but not to the other. In the case of robots, we would prejudge the question by asking, for example, whether an M-theory or a C-theory would be more appropriate to explain a robot's intentionally making an insulting remark to the key-punch operator whom it considers to be rather stupid. This of course presupposes one of the explanatory frameworks being considered and is therefore an unacceptable formulation of the question.

What is required of us, then, is to describe the phenomenon in question in terms neutral to the alternative conceptual schemes being discussed. I leave it as an open question whether a description neutral relative to the given pair of conceptual schemes in question will be available in all such cases, although I see no reason to suppose the contrary. If there are in fact cases in which no description is available which is schematically-neutral, i.e., which allows for the possible appropriateness of more than one conceptual scheme, then the answer is implicit in the question. But this is a secondary set of issues/problems. (I will leave the question of whether there are in fact any such cases as an open question.)

In the above-given example, for example, there is such a scheme-neutral description. We have, that is, the description of a robot's printing a card which when decoded reads, "Any other stupid ideas?" (This explanandum could, prima facie, be explained by either an M-theory or a C-theory.)

There are, however, several reasons for supposing that the criterion of relative simplicity will be an inadequate one. Firstly, it is not an obvious truth that it is possible to judge relative simplicity of explanations made in two conceptually different theories. Quine claims, for example, "Simplicity is not easy to define. But it may be expected, whatever it is, to be relative to the texture of a conceptual scheme."[3] But partially because Quine says nothing in support of this thesis, I do not hold this position to be an established, or in fact, an acceptable one.

---

[3]"On Simple Theories of a Complex World," *Synthese,* vol. 15, No. 1 (1963), p. 103.

A more serious problem is the following. Even assuming that one can judge relative simplicity between explanations in two different conceptual schemes, there is excellent reason to believe that the more acceptable conceptual scheme will not necessarily be the one which provides the simpler explanation. The simpler one might rightly be rejected, for example, for being incompatible with the bulk of accepted knowledge, for being extremely unenlightening, for being self-contradictory, etc., etc.[4] We will give a more adequate presentation of G-factors (factors which provide justification for accepting a given conceptual scheme's applicability to a given phenomenon), below.

Before that, however, there is one issue in the philosophy of science whose resolution might be held to suggest a resolution to the present problem of giving grounds for choosing between competing conceptual schemes in reference to a certain phenomenon. The issue is that of reductionism, the claim that the laws and propositions of one given study or science,[5] S1, may be derivable from (A) those of a second study or science, S2, together with (B) certain "bridge principles" (Hempel's phrase) which amount to translation functions or rules which determine the replacement of statements in the vocabulary of S1 by others in the vocabulary of S2.[6] Under these conditions, S1 is said to be reducible to S2. This is, of course, *not* to say that what is described by a claim using the vocabulary of S1 is "really" only the phenomenon described by the claim in the vocabulary

---

[4]For the basis of twenty criteria for determining whether a given theory is an improvement on a competing theory, see M. Bunge, "The Weight of Simplicity in the Construction and Assaying of Scientific Theories," *Philosophy of Science*, vol. 28 (1961), pp. 129-149. Extremely importantly, *not* all of these twenty are relevant factors in choosing between two competing *conceptual schemes*, even if we accept Bunge's claim that all twenty are relevant in evaluating competing *theories* (employing the same kind of concepts).

[5]I.e., a systematized field of inquiry. (Here 'science' is being used as equivalent to the German 'Wissenschaft'.)

[6]This statement of reductionism is based on the discussion in Hempel, *Philosophy of Natural Science* (Englewood Cliffs, N.J., Prentice-Hall, Inc., 1966), esp. pp. 102-105.

of S2 gotten by these reduction- or bridge- or translation-rules.[7]

One might hold, however, that if a given conceptual scheme C1 is reducible in this sense to a second conceptual scheme C2, then the more appropriate conceptual scheme to use to describe phenomena which are at first held to be explicable by either or both of the two is C2, and not C1. This position would hold, that is, that the reduced-to conceptual scheme, C2, is more appropriate to explain phenomena than the reduced-from conceptual scheme, C1.

This claim of course, suggests that if C1 is reducible to C2, then C2 is more appropriate to *all* phenomena which are prima facie structurable in terms of either C2 or C1. This position is in the programmatic spirit of some of the works of the logical positivists (e.g., Carnap, *The Unity of Science*[8]) when applied to the parallel problem of choosing between scientific theories, and also might be read into some writings outside of the positivist school. Consider, for example, the visionary comment of Ziff: "But fortunately conceptual decay is the order of the day. . . . Our intellectual concepts, [such as] thinking, planning, experimenting, all are tottering. . . . [O]ther plain concepts are likely to survive. And possibly in time, if the race lingers on, adequate translation functions will be found for the survivors."[9]

I take it, however, that this position is not altogether acceptable. Its superficial reasonableness relies heavily upon the supposition that when a phenomenon is describable in a framework which is reducible to a second framework, all that is "really" the case is that phenomenon described in the latter framework. But this is, of course, just one more formulation of the reductionist fallacy mentioned above.

It seems, however, that there are some reasonable grounds underlying this position (especially as embodied in the Ziff

---

[7]Hospers calls this invalid implication the reductive fallacy, or the nothing-but fallacy. (*An Introduction to Philosophical Analysis* (Englewood. Cliffs, N.J., Prentice-Hall, Inc., 1965), pp. 302-303.)

[8]Trans. M. Black (London, Kegan Paul, Trench, Trubner & Co., Ltd., 1934).

[9]"The Simplicity of Other Minds," *Journal of Philosophy*, vol. 62, (1965), Sect. 17, p. 584.

quote just above). And these are the following. Let us suppose that some F1 (a given conceptual framework) is reducible to some F2 (some other conceptual framework.) (By way of illustration, one might look at F1 as biology and F2 as physics, but this is not necessary for the point I am making.) If all of the members of a discipline which is interested in explaining phenomena usually (up until time t_1) described in terms of F1 accept, at t_1, the reducibility of F1 to F2, then analyses and investigations in that discipline may very well be radically altered. Reformulation of problems from F1 in the concepts of F2 may occur. Sophistication may then occur in the theory involving F2, while that involving F1 may stagnate, remain clumsy, imprecise, etc. As a result of this, it may one day be reasonable to hold that explanations in F2 are then much more sophisticated, precise, etc., than explanations were at previous times using F1. One might even argue that at that time F2 will be a more adequate, illuminating, systematically more acceptable (and, correlatively, scientifically more acceptable) framework to use in theoretical contexts than F1. It does *not* follow from this last claim, however, that F2 will therefore be more acceptable than F1 in all contexts. (Such a fallacy, if it deserved a name, might be called the disciplinarians' fallacy.)

Such investigations, as just noted, *may* strongly influence one's position on the applicability of particular schemes to given phenomena. To introduce just one relevant possibility: In the case of M-theories vs. C-theories, the development of bridge laws joining an M-theory to a neurological theory may bring people to the position that the mind is a property of a highly structured energy system (in this case, electrochemical in nature).[10]

---

[10]The exact way in which these bridge laws would be formulated is still open, but contra Bruce Goldberg, "The Correspondence Hypothesis," *Philosophical Review*, vol. 77, No. 4 (October, 1968), pp. 438-454, let me suggest that neurological states or processes will probably be correlated with states of consciousness (paradigm: a sensation such as of pain) rather than to a thought or even to thinking a thought. Goldberg's article argues only against correlating *thoughts* with brain states, and not against correlating *sensations* with neurological states or processes.

If this view is taken and such bridge laws are accepted correlating sensations with neurological states or processes, then there will be rather highly theoretical reasons for holding that complex computers or robots also have consciousness. For if their circuitry parallels neurological structure and their states or processes do also (if, for example, the parallel structures are carrying the same electric (electro-chemical) currents), the bridge laws will lead one to conclude that the corresponding state of consciousness has obtained in both cases.[11] To speculate, this would perhaps suggest that it is the robot's circuitry and the brain which are conscious rather than the robot and the person per se. It would also involve, of course, a rejection of T (introduced in the preceding chapter).

Yet there are situations in which the imprecision, etc., are quite acceptable considering the purposes at hand. (The case of using a crude tripartite soul or mind as formulated by Plato, discussed in the preceding chapter, in a situation outside of the psychologist's lab or the psychiatrist's office might be rather appropriate, easy to understand, vague and short enough for the triviality of the general tenor of the context, etc.) To suppose that the most sophisticated theory is the best for all purposes is, it seem clear, somewhat unreasonable.

If this is so, then the fact that a conceptual scheme C1 is reducible to some second conceptual scheme, C2, is relevant to (A), the question of whether C1 will be (more) appropriate to extremely complex investigation, description, and explanation of phenomena also analyzable in terms of C2, or whether C2 will. But this question, although related to the question we are primarily interested in, is nonetheless to be distinguished from it. *This* question is (B), the question of whether it is in *any* context (more) appropriate to use C1 for the description (and explanation) of phenomena also analyzable in terms of C2, or whether C2 is always (more) appropriate. Even if we assume that C1's being reducible to C2 provides us with an answer to (A), it does *not* provide one to (B).

---

[11]Cf. Kenneth Sayre, *Recognition: A Study in the Philosophy of Artificial Intelligence*, Notre Dame, University of Notre Dame Press, 1965.

Were we primarily interested in why one of two frameworks, both of which are applicable to a given phenomenon, is in fact chosen in some contexts (but not in others), we would be interested at this point in seeing precisely what determines this choice. It would then be appropriate to say more about what these determining factors are: It would be just a beginning to say that F1 is chosen over F2 in a given context because of the degree of preciseness of description, the range of control over the phenomenon the people involved are interested in obtaining, the people's depth of understanding of the two frameworks, etc., the air of lightness or seriousness desired in the discussion, the depth of understanding and appreciation of the phenomenon desired, etc., etc.

But as this is not our primary interest, I will let what I have just said suffice, and turn to our problem, which we can now state, having distinguished it from the above-mentioned one, as follows:

What factors are relevant to our deciding whether a given conceptual scheme can be appropriately used to describe, explain, etc., a given entity or phenomenon? In the discussion which is to follow, I will suggest several factors which I hold to be relevant to such a decision (whether a given conceptual scheme is applicable to a given entity or phenomenon). The factors to be proposed are such that by considering them, reasons can be generated relevant to this decision. Each of these reasons will make it more (or: less) reasonable to claim that the scheme is applicable.

This should not lead us to a possible confusion. If we know that a given X-scheme is applicable to some y, and then decide that an M-theory is clearly *in*applicable to that y, then it follows that the given (applicable) X-scheme is *not* an M-theory. Following what has been said, we can say that the reasons generated on the basis of the factors to be presented make it more (or: less) reasonable to say that the X-scheme is an M-theory. But we *cannot* say that these reasons show that the X-scheme is an M-theory to a lesser (or greater) degree. There are degrees of reasonableness in claiming that some scheme is an M-theory, *but* there are *not* degrees of being an M-theory. Once it is determined on the basis of such reasons that a given scheme is an M-theory, these factors (and reasons thereon generated) have served their function.

The final determination of whether a scheme is applicable, then, depends on the degree to which the reasons which each of these factors provides, either for or against supposing a conceptual scheme to be conceptually appropriate to a given entity, counter-balance the reasons each other factor provides. At this stage of formulation, it is rather premature to suggest any calculus for combining and balancing these various reasons. In addition to this limitation, I am not convinced that the list which follows is at all complete. But it will suggest the lines along which one might give an argument to substantiate or ground one's position on whether or not an M-theory is conceptually appropriate to robots. Why, then, accept or reject a given conceptual scheme as applicable to a given entity?

G-factor I. The conceptual scheme is patently internally inconsistent. That is, if we attempt to draw up statements which incorporate the central concepts of the conceptual scheme and in doing so are able to draw many obvious and mutually contradictory conclusions, we have excellent reason (the best?) to suppose that the conceptual scheme is simply an unworkable one, one inadequate for any phenomenon. This, if it were to obtain, would be reason to reject the conceptual scheme in question in toto, and, a fortiori, to reject it in the context in question. I must add, however, that this is a rather secondary factor, since *serious* contenders will have been accepted by that point as internally consistent.

Note that G-factor I is related to the question of whether the conceptual scheme in question is at all acceptable. In most of the interesting cases, however, the conceptual scheme will probably be in use for some range of phenomena other than that at stake when the question of its applicability to some entity is raised. Rather, then, than continuing with grounds for rejecting conceptual schemes in toto (see Bunge, *op. cit.*, for several more), let us turn to those factors which are relevant once it has been established or simply given that the conceptual scheme can be acceptably applied to some other entities.

G-factor II. There are some states, behavior, etc. of the entity in question which are prima facie explicable in terms of the conceptual scheme. This in effect requires that some reason be given to support the original contention that the conceptual scheme is applicable to the entity in question. This requirement is for some rather general, weak evidence which can be interpreted as showing that the entity has the kind of properties embodied in the concepts of the conceptual scheme. If no such evidence can be presented, the case for this conceptual scheme's being applicable is much weaker.

It is for such a reason that we are justified in refusing to talk, for example, of rocks as MPs. For, among other possible evidence, there is very little, if anything, they do which gives us reason to suppose them to possess minds. They do not express wishes, desires, beliefs, emotions, etc. Nor do they seem to act on the basis of desires, etc. Letting moss grow on itself is hardly overwhelming evidence for the attribution of a want to a rock, nor is free-falling at thirty-two feet per second per second. A rock is too passive to be an MP. (Even prima facie, we would immediately have to attribute paralysis to it. But it is difficult to know just what this would amount to in rocks. For in other cases of paralysis-attribution, other members of the kind are *not* paralysed. This is of course *not* the case with rocks. This consideration suggests a third factor in such questioning (cf., below, under factor III).

Before raising this third factor, however, it is important to see a major implication of this second one. If II *is* acceptable, then what follows is that there is empirical information which is relevant to the status of certain conceptual claims.

We say, for example, that a rock cannot (a logical or conceptual 'cannot') think about Vienna. That this is so depends on the fact that a conceptual framework with mental notions as its central ones is simply inapplicable to rocks. But if II, above, is accepted, then this in turn is a function of the empirical evidence, or lack thereof, for supposing this conceptual framework to be applicable. Therefore, empirical evidence is ultimately relevant to the conceptual claim made above, viz., that rocks cannot think about Vienna.

Note, for example, how our presuppositions about the inapplicability of a mentalistic conceptual scheme to rocks would be brought into question if there were to be widespread, well-accredited reports that rocks all over the world were heard to make noises heard as speech in different languages (depending where the rocks were) to the effect that the rocks were tired, had grown lazy, wished they could move without being thrown or dropped, could get the moss off their tops every so often, etc. If things were *very* different, we might reject our conceptual truth (that rocks cannot think about Vienna).[12]

Since, however, there is no such evidence in support of the supposition that a mentalistic conceptual scheme is applicable to rocks, the case of rocks is a rather obvious case in which to refuse the applicability of an M-theory.

G-factor III. There is or is not reason to suppose that a revision of the central statements embodying the concepts of the conceptual scheme will be required if the conceptual scheme is held to be applicable to the entity in question.

Let me explain this factor more fully. We accept certain statements made using the vocabulary of a certain conceptual scheme. These statements provide us with an understanding of the conceptual scheme's concepts. It is, in fact, in virtue of their presence in such statements that the concepts are significant. If we suppose that this conceptual scheme is applicable to a given entity, then it will perhaps be the case that there will

---

[12]If this is correct, then we have something to say which might interest logicians and philosophers of religion. For the above discussion gives reason to suppose that it can be necessarily true that s (where 's' is a dummy variable for some statement), and yet it not be necessarily true that it is necessarily true that s. And this in turn amounts to saying, where 'N' is to be read "it is necessarily the case that", that Ns does not entail NNs. It suggests, correlatively, that one *cannot* deduce that it is necessarily true that God exists necessarily from the supposition that God exists necessarily (*even* if this latter is or were acceptable).

be no need whatsoever to revise the defining statements in order to account for this entity's characteristics. But this is not necessarily the case. Assuming that an ant, for example, is an MP might require us to revise some of the statements which delineate the way in which wants, beliefs, etc., manifest themselves, how they are generated or changed; in short, their characteristics. We might, that is, find it necessary to alter many presuppositions about the central notions of the scheme. If this is done to a great enough degree, we will be involved in a *modification of the scheme's concepts*.[13] If this is necessary, then there is reason to suppose that the conceptual scheme (as it was) is, in fact, not applicable to this entity.

The degree to which one must modify a conceptual scheme's presuppositions to accommodate a given entity to the descriptions, explanations, etc., available within that scheme is, of course, an empirical matter. (Cf. factor II.) In addition, it is also conceivable that one may have to modify one's conceptual scheme to a different degree under different conditions, e.g., if the entity in question changes its own properties. This third factor, consequently, is obviously one for which different empirical conditions will make it more or less reasonable to claim the conceptual scheme's applicability to the entity in question.

G-factor IV. Considering the conceptual scheme to be applicable to the entity in question provides a classification which is for independent factors (i.e., independent of the above-listed G-factors I, II, and III) reasonable or unreasonable. What might

---

[13]Minor changes in central assumptions and major changes in peripheral assumptions may change a theory to such a small degree—I am not assuming any sophisticated metric of change here—that no change in the theory's concepts is brought about. In this way, one aspect of some recent discussions seems to amount to a dialectic about whether certain changes are sufficiently central or major to count as generating modified concepts. (E.g., Malcolm on dreaming (*Dreaming*, London, Routledge & Kegan Paul, Ltd., 1959) and Putnam on Malcolm on Dreaming ("Dreaming and 'Depth Grammar'," pp. 211-235 in R. J. Butler, ed., *Analytical Philosophy*, First Series, Oxford, Basil Blackwell & Mott, Ltd., 1962)). I do not know how to resolve this issue in any very convincing way.

make this unreasonable? I will provide just one detailed illustration (perhaps there are more to be given). The illustration will depend on my establishing two points, both of which are rather harmless—trivial, in fact. Together, however, they have rather interesting consequences.

The first of the points is a claim held to be analytic by several prominent ethical philosophers (e.g., Hare,[14] Nowell-Smith,[15] Baier, [16] C. I. Lewis[17]). The claim is that all members of the same class deserve, at least prima facie, the same considerations which any arbitrary member of the class deserves in virtue of its being in the class, and that one who treats any member of this class in a given way deserves the same respect, disrespect, etc., as he does for his treating any other member in that way. If there is no question of consideration relevant at all, this claim is somewhat empty but still acceptable. We shall take, however, a case in which such consideration is relevant.

The second point to be made is the claim that all entities to which a given conceptual scheme is applicable belong to the same set or class. In the case of those entities to whom an M-theory is applicable, the class involved is that of all MPs.

If we consider these two claims conjointly, we can derive the following consideration: All entities to which a given conceptual scheme is applicable deserve, at least prima facie, the same considerations given any arbitrary one in virtue of its having the given conceptual scheme applicable to it.

Note that insofar as some entity is taken *not* to be something (*not* to be an instance of a particular kind), the considerations made to that kind of thing may well be withheld from the given entity. Thus we have the following report of Bateson's:

---

[14]*The Language of Morals* (New York, Oxford University Press, 1964), e.g., Section 10.2 (esp. p. 153).

[15]*Ethics* (London, Penguin Books, Ltd., 1965), e.g., Chap. 12, Section 5 (esp. p. 177).

[16]*The Moral Point of View: A Rational Basis of Ethics* (Ithaca, Cornell University Press, 1958), e.g., Chap. 8, Section 3 (esp. p. 195).

[17]*The Ground and Nature of the Right* (New York, Columbia University Press, 1958), e.g., pp. 79, 86, 93.

The late Doctor Stutterheim, Government Archeologist in Java, used to tell the following story: Somewhat before the advent of the white man, there was a storm on the Javanese coast in the neighborhood of one of the capitals. After the storm the people went down to the beach and found, washed up by the waves and almost dead, a large white monkey of unknown species. The religious experts explained that this monkey had been a member of the court of Beroena, the God of the Sea, and that for some offense the monkey had been cast out by the god whose anger was expressed in the storm. The Rajah gave orders that the white monkey from the sea should be kept alive, chained to a certain stone. This was done. Doctor Stutterheim told me that he had seen the stone and that, roughly scratched on it in Latin, Dutch, and English were the name of a man and a statement of his shipwreck. Apparently this trilingual sailor never established verbal communication with his captors. He was surely unaware of the premises in their minds which labeled him as a white monkey and therefore not a potential recipient of verbal messages: it probably never occurred to him that they could doubt his humanity. He may have doubted theirs.[18]

Furthermore, if we consider the particular case of a mentalistic conceptual scheme, we can derive from the above-derived consideration: All MPs deserve, at least prima facie, the same considerations given any arbitrary one in virtue of its being an MP.

Are there any interesting consequences which can be drawn from this? Let us for a moment consider the claim that wine

---

[18]Footnote 2 on pp. 204f., Gregory Bateson, "Information and Codification: A Philosophical Approach," in J. Ruesch and G. Bateson, *Communication: The Social Matrix of Psychiatry* (New York, W. W. Norton & Co., Inc., 1951).

is a sentient being.[19] If something is a sentient being, of course, it is an MP (cf. chapter one.)

This claim then, requires that a mentalistic conceptual scheme can be appropriately applied to wines, i.e., that wines are MPs. But if we accept the claim about wines now under consideration, then it follows that wines deserve, at least prima facie, the same considerations given any arbitrarily chosen MP in virtue of its being an MP.

Let us suppose, then, that a somewhat considerate individual is kind to a stray dog, treats it gently, stops others from kicking it, etc., on the sole grounds that it has feelings, is sensitive, can be hurt by maltreatment, etc., i.e., that it is an MP. It would follow then, at least prima facie, that this individual would deserve the same acclaim, respect, etc., due to him because of his treatment of the stray dog were he to treat a wine in a parallel fashion. (This might amount to his handling it carefully, storing it at the appropriate temperature, serving it with the appropriate foods, etc.)

What can we say about this claim? It might be profitable to compare it with a similar claim such as the following. It is at least prima facie the case that this individual would deserve the same acclaim, respect, etc., due to him because of his treatment of the stray dog were he to treat some red-winged blackbird in a parallel fashion.

There seems, importantly, to be a difference between these two claims. How do they differ, and on what grounds can we justify our holding there to be this difference?

The second claim but not the first seems to be reasonable. That is, if someone claims to respect the above individual for

---

[19]Compare what is being said here with the structure of the argument in the following article suggesting that wine is a living being: "Unlike whiskey or other distilled spirits, wine is a living thing, and it should be treated the same commonsensical way as living creatures. People become sick with abrupt changes of temperature; so does wine. After severe shaking or protracted voyaging a wine, like a person, needs a rest. Otherwise, it will arrive at your table tired, and taste so." (F. S. Wildman, Jr., "A Wine Tour of France, part I: Introduction," *Gourmet*, vol. 28, No. 2 (Feb., 1967), p. 32.)

treating the stray dog as he did, if that individual were to treat a red-winged blackbird in a parallel fashion, and yet that someone refused to admit respect for the individual for *this* treatment, it would seem prima facie appropriate (for ethical reasons) for that someone to justify this apparent discrimination. On the other hand, were these same circumstances to arise in reference to a wine rather than a red-winged blackbird, it would seem prima facie that no question of justification actually arises.

Why is this so? In order to explain this, we are in need of the concept of a normatively-operant classification. A normatively-operant classification is a classification which is held to generate a class of individuals such that membership in that class provides for some individual the prima facie right to the same considerations as any other member of that class is held to have.

Thus, whether a classification is a normatively-operant one depends on the group which is employing the classification in question, and, more exactly, on the context in which the classification is to be employed.

Thus, for example, baldness (a classification which generates the class of individuals all of whom are bald) is, I assume, not a normatively-operant one in the Church's papal elections. That is, suppose that two Catholics, A and B, are both bald, and that both are being considered by the electing body in an election of the next pope. Suppose further that A has just been described as an extremely fine candidate, as one who would make an excellent pope. If baldness is not a normatively-operant classification in this context, as I assume that it is not, then it would be held to be simply *irrelevant* for someone to claim that B, too, must be, prima facie, an excellent candidate for pope since he too is bald. (One can imagine, however, other circumstances, in which baldness *would* be a normatively-operant classification.)

Conversely, for example, obedience is a normatively-operant classification in the evaluation of a child's manners in much of bourgeois society. That is, if both of two children, A and B, are obedient (e.g., to their parents, their teachers, older people in general), and A has just been described as well-mannered, it would be relevant to continue by arguing that B too is (somewhat) well-mannered, since B too is obedient. Even if being obedient is not held to be conclusive evidence for the claim that some child is well-mannered, it is held to be relevant. (As in the above case, other circumstances can be imagined in which obedience would *not* be a normatively-operant classification.)

Let us now see how this notion sheds light on our problem of the wine and the red-winged blackbird. We are assuming, as was stated in the original presentation of the problem, that being an MP is a normatively-operant classification in the evaluation of treatment of other beings. That is, we are assuming that the group of people in question finds it relevant to evaluate an individual (partially) in terms of that individual's treatment of MPs.

On the other hand, it seems highly counter-intuitive to claim that an individual in such a context would be evaluated (as to whether he is kind, considerate, sensitive brutal, inconsiderate, etc., etc.) — even partially — on the basis of his treatment of a wine. What this amounts to is that how an individual treats wines seems prima facie to be irrelevant to the evaluation of that individual as kind, etc. Note, in contrast to this, that how he treats wines might be held to be relevant to questions of his aesthetic (gustatory) appreciation, his savoir faire, his sophistication, etc. We can divide the kinds of normative judgments about such an individual that might be made, into two groups. The first of these concerns that individual's kindness, considerateness, sensitivity, brutality, inconsiderateness, etc. The second concerns his aesthetic (gustatory) appreciation, his savoir faire, his sophistication, etc. This first set, which could be supplemented, consists of those judgments which employ notions used in ethical evaluation. The second set, which could also be supplemented, consists of those which employ notions used in social evaluation.[20] We can say, then, that intuitively, how one treats a wine might be relevant to a determination of one's social character[20] (whether desirable or not) but *not* of one's moral character (whether desirable or not).

Yet we *would* hold his treatment of a red-winged blackbird to be reflective of his moral character, i.e., *would* hold it to be relevant to a determination of his moral character. Why is this so?

What is operant in this problem is a certain presupposition, viz., that wines are in fact not MPs. If this is so, then it is of course unacceptable to argue that one deserves the same respect, etc., for his kind treatment of a wine as for one's kind treatment of a stray dog, even assuming that the stray dog is so treated merely because it is a sentient being. For the moral principle in question is only relevant when the two objects of treatment are members of a (perhaps ethically) normatively-operant classification. But the normatively-operant classification here, viz., that of being an MP, does not apply to wines. Therefore, we hold the treatment of a wine to be irrelevant to our evaluation of one's ethical character. Since, however, we assume that red-winged blackbirds *are* MPs, we hold *that* argument (that one deserves, prima facie, the same respect, etc., for one's treatment of red-winged blackbirds as for that of stray dogs since they are both MPs) to be sound.

This difference depends on the fact that if one holds a classification to be an ethically or socially or other normatively-operant one, and also holds that two individuals, A, and B, are both members of the class generated by that classification, then, if one is not to be inconsistent, one must also hold that A and B have, prima facie, the same ethical or social or other normative status (but this claim is acceptable only if A and B are members of that class).

This fact has, however, a somewhat interesting implication. In a society in which a given classification is (at times) a normatively-operant one, there are certain immediate normative

---

[20]That there are (presumably pompous) individuals who bother to classify others in such terms is both sad and humorous. The distinction introduced nonetheless remains.

implications to classifying a given (kind of) entity in the class generated by that normatively-operant classification. And in some situations, these normative implications may be in conflict with certain other normative presuppositions.

In the case of the wine, e.g., the presupposition that how one treats a wine is irrelevant to an evaluation of that individual's ethical character (even if it might not be irrelevant to one of his social character) is in conflict with the ethically normatively-operant classification of being an MP, given the single added supposition that wines are (now) being classified as MPs. More exactly, one cannot consistently maintain all three of the following: (a) How an individual treats an MP in virtue of its being an MP is relevant to an ethical evaluation of that individual, (b) How an individual treats a wine is irrelevant to an ethical evaluation of that individual, and, (c) Wine is an MP.

Thus, if one maintains both (a) and (b), and then comes to the opinion that (c) is true, then one has accepted inconsistent claims. Or, somewhat differently, if one accepts (a), then there will be certain immediate ethical implications in accepting (c).

And it can be seen from these considerations that insofar as the presentation of a conceptual scheme is (can be) a prelude to the adoption of the concepts therein for the generation of normatively-operant classications, a normative stand can be suggested in a presentation of purely conceptual claims.[21] We should examine this point in a more general way. The claims being made are based on one single instance of something more general. And that is the following: There are certain operant classifications in a given society such that one who accepts the practices of that group will find appropriate a certain treatment

---

[21]This is, I think, responsible for part of the force of Nietzsche's insistence on determining the morality a philosopher will ultimately attempt to justify in understanding, etc., his statements. Cf. "Indeed, if one would explain how the abstrusest metaphysical claims of a philosopher really come about, it is always well (and wise) to ask first: at what morality does all this (does *he*) aim?" (*Beyond Good and Evil*, trans. W. Kaufmann (New York, Vintage Books, 1966), Sect. 6, his emphasis and parentheses. See also Sections 8, 289, etc.)

of and attitude towards entities which are members of the class generated by one of those classifications. In such a case, the practical (in Kant's sense of 'practical') implications of holding that a given individual is or is not in that class may be immense. In the above case, the operant classification was that of being an MP, and the context was one of ethical evaluation, and so the implications were of course of an ethical nature. But this is only one of *many* contexts. (Consider, e.g., social, aesthetic, economic (e.g., consider the concept of a barterable piece of goods with reference to the single question of whether human beings are members of the set thereby generated), religious (e.g., in a society allowing religious freedom, consider the concept of a religion with reference to the single question of whether Leary's League for Spiritual Discovery is a member of that set), political (e.g., in a society in which Communist activities are illegal, the concept of a Communist-front organization with reference to the single question of whether the Lincoln Brigade is a member of such a set), legal (e.g., in a society allowing federal government power over inter-state but not over intra-state commerce, the concept of inter-state commerce with reference to the question of whether growing crops only for one's personal use or for that of friends in the same town is a member of that set), etc., etc.)

In the light of this fact, we should ask the following question: Is the question of how one should deal with a given entity logically prior to that of whether that entity is a member of a given set of entities or not? Differently stated, there are two interrelated questions, viz., (1) How should an X be treated?, and, (2) Is this X a y? Now, the present question is: Is the answer to (2) ever a function of the answer to (1)? Or, is it always either that the two answers are independent of one another or else that the answer to (1) is a function of the answer to (2)? For A to be a function of (or independent of) B is, of course, for B to be relevant (or irrelevant) to the determination of what A is. If it is the latter question which is answered affirmatively, then an incompatibility between a statement of class inclusion (e.g., wine is an MP, i.e., wine is a member of the class of all MPs) using a normatively-operant classification (being an MP) and an accepted practice (e.g., ethical evaluation of an individual is *never* in terms of his treatment of wines) should be resolved at the expense of the accepted practice. But if it is the former which is affirmatively answered, then the way in which Xs are held to be appropriately considered may in *some* cases be relevant in our then determining whether Xs are a certain kind of being. If this former *is* answered affirmatively, then the fourth factor above (viz., IV: Considering the conceptual scheme to be applicable to the entity in question provides a classification which is for independent factors reasonable or unreasonable) has been established and can join the other three. If, however, it is answered negatively, a case of such unreasonableness (as referred to in the statement of the fourth factor) can be only symptomatic of inconsistency elsewhere, and *cannot itself* be a factor in our determining whether the conceptual scheme in question is applicable to the (kind of) entity.

It is essential, then, to answer this one final set of questions. At first, the obvious answer seems to be that the answer to (2) is never a function of the answer to (1), i.e., that the answer to the first question of this pair is negative (and that to the second is affirmative).

What might be said in favor of the intuitively obvious answer to these questions? The answer in focus, as mentioned above, is that the answer to the question of whether some X is a y is never a function of the answer to the question of how some X should be treated. And in support of this position it could be argued that:

To ask whether an X is a y (e.g., whether a wine is an MP, whether a Socialist Labor Party local is a Communist-front organization, etc.) is to ask something about what *Xs* are like, what *Xs'* characteristics are, etc. It is not to ask about *us;* it is not to ask how *we* feel about Xs, how *we* think it is appropriate for us to treat Xs,, etc. Furthermore, it seems that how we feel about Xs depends on many factors such as how we think we should act toward Xs, how much we want to do what we think is socially, etc. appropriate, how we react to Xs, etc. Importantly, these factors (how we think we should act toward Xs, &c.) are determined not only by what Xs are like, but also by what we are like. For how we react to Xs, what we take Xs to be like, etc., depends (partly) on what Xs are like (and (partly) on what we are like). This is a genetic point, but a parallel point can be made in terms of the relation between characteristics and attitudes. That is, we generally assume, first of all, that in justifying one's attitudes toward Xs, it is relevant to discuss Xs' characteristics or properties. We assume, that is, that what attitudes are appropriately had toward Xs depends on what Xs are like. Secondly, we assume that what Xs are like does *not* depend on what attitudes are appropriately had toward Xs. The answers to questions about attitudes toward Xs seem to depend on what Xs are. (This can be summed up by saying that characteristics are logically prior to attitudes, but I shall not rely too heavily on the notion of logical priority.)

The intuitive appeal of this position depends on, I think, a certain kind of naive realism, viz., the belief that learning about the world consists of observing different entities, observing just what they are or are not, observing just what characteristics they do or do not have, and perhaps also of systematizing the facts thus gleaned by observation. This notion does in fact seem to be adequate to account for the genesis of most of what we assume to be knowledge about the world, viz., that large portion which reflects the attitude of scientists in what Kuhn considers is found in periods of "normal science"[22] (when one set of scientific theories is considered to be rather well-embedded, with no essentially insoluble paradoxes or problems, and with no weighty alternative theories vying for acceptance by the scientific community, however that is to be identified).

There are, however, situations in which this model is inadequate, i.e., whose logic this model does not illuminate. Some situations are such that if one uses this model to describe and explain them, one will have less of an understanding of the

---

[22]Cf. his *The Structure of Scientific Revolutions* (Chicago, The University of Chicago Press, 1966), esp. chapters 3, 4.

situations, will not see the most important and illuminating interrelations between the various constituents which compose the situations, etc., than had one used another model (viz., the one to be sketched presently).

The model to be sketched blurs the distinction between invention and discovery,[23] or, differently stated, shows situations in which a sharp distinction cannot be validly made. The model will, hopefully, allow for those situations in which the distinction is fruitful, but will take them to be special cases, i.e., will take it that there *are* such other situations.

In most situations, then, a given conceptual scheme is in force in a given community. Furthermore, the range of applicability of the scheme is settled, and no problematic instances arise. In the case of a mentalistic framework, for example, this situation would be one in which it was clear in all cases that arise whether the framework is appropriately applicable to a given entity. There are, at this time, no entities considered by the community for classification in reference to the framework in question which are theoretically important borderline cases. This period can be likened to that of "normal science" in Kuhn's sense.

At another period, however, entities are considered for which the given framework is neither clearly applicable or clearly inapplicable. Furthermore, these entities reveal a certain indefiniteness of the framework in its present condition. (In the case of a mentalistic framework, the cases of "brutes" (animals other than human beings) and robots prove revealing because they require us to examine our grounds for classification.)[24] Such problematic cases are also theoretically important because they might suggest grounds on which various problematic claims can be resolved. (E.g., in the example, the issue of behaviorism.)

In addition, and most importantly, there may be practical

---

[23]Cf. Kuhn, *op. cit.*, 52: "That distinction between discovery and invention or between fact and theory will, however, immediately prove to be exceedingly superficial." See the following pages of that work for his discussion.

[24]Compare this with Kuhn's discussion of anomaly and crisis and their relation to the emergence of new scientific theories, esp. Kuhn, *op. cit.*, chapters 6 and 7.

reasons why one *must* determine whether the framework is to be held to be applicable to the entity in question (e.g., in question of classification in certain cases brought before the United States Supreme Court). It is in just such problematic cases that the sharp distinction between discovery and invention, or between finding out and deciding or legislating, cannot be maintained. (The word 'determine' in the sentence above beginning "In addition" might easily have been replaced by 'legislate'.) For here one cannot determine whether a framework is applicable just by observing what the entity in question is like. And that is because the entity has those characteristics which would make it a problematic case. (In those cases where the answer is not obvious it will not suffice to look to the obvious for an answer.) That is, our understanding of the framework is such that the grounds obtained by determining what the entity is like are insufficient to allow us to determine whether the framework is applicable or not. (If one were Wittgensteinian one could say one it at a point in his performance where the rule he is using no longer tells him what to do, which of the vying alternative actions are acceptable and which are not.)

At such times, three obvious alternatives present themselves. The first of these is to refrain from making any claims which suggest, state, or presuppose that the framework is applicable or *in*applicable to the entity. An interesting situation is one in which a decision is definitely required, for practical (e.g., social, legal, etc.) reasons. In such a situation, this first alternative may well be found to be *un*acceptable.

The second alternative is to decide arbitrarily that the framework is applicable or inapplicable, that is, to decide without attempting to base one's decision on any grounds.

But there is also a third alternative, viz., to decide whether the framework is applicable on the basis of justifying reasons. To state what this decision (in both the second and third alternatives) is, we can say that it is *not* exactly a decision that the framework *is* applicable or inapplicable, but rather a decision that it is more *reasonable* to *extend* the framework's applicability to covering this (kind of) entity. If we realize this, then the question of whether a framework is applicable to a given entity can be REPLACED by that of whether it is more reasonable to apply the framework to that (kind of) entity than not to.[25]

The fact that in many cases it is extremely obvious whether a conceptual scheme is applicable to a given entity (or not) can be seen on this model as being the result of the fact that it is rather obvious (in such cases) that it is more reasonable (not) to apply the framework to that entity than not to apply it (then to apply it). If this is so, then it is understandable both why the question of how we treat Xs is usually irrelevant to establishing which conceptual schemes are appropriate to Xs (viz., because other reasons would dwarf the logical weight of the answer to this question), and also why the answer to such a question is relevant to the establishing of which conceptual schemes are appropriate to Xs (or, in a vocabulary which is somewhat obfuscating in this context: of what Xs are like) in the most problematic cases.

If what has just been said is correct, then we can say the following. The first three factors listed above can be appealed to in a justification of the claim that a given conceptual scheme is or is not applicable to a given kind of entity or phenomenon, X. When, however, it is necessary to hold that a given scheme is or is not applicable to a given kind of entity or phenomenon, X, and it is also the case that one cannot *clearly* justify one's position by these first three factors, then one must come to a certain realization. This realization is that the conceptual scheme in question neither (a) clearly applies to this X, nor (b) clearly does not apply to this X. In such a case, one must decide whether to modify the scheme slightly so as to include or so as to exclude this X in the scheme's (new) range of applicability. One must decide, that is, to extend the scheme's applicability so as to include or so as to exclude the given X therefrom. In making the applicability precise where it has been imprecise, one is

---

[25]This has a parallel in the evolution of science. E.g., Kuhn, *op. cit.*, "A decision between alternative ways of practicing science is called for, and in the circumstances that decision must be based less on past achievement than on future promise." (pp. 156f.)

slightly modifying the scheme, but in certain contexts this may be required.

The fourth factor will provide grounds, then, for the claim that a given scheme should be held applicable or not to a given X. It will be appropriate to appeal to this fourth factor *only* in those situations in which one must replace the question (A) Is a Y-scheme (obviously) applicable to Xs?, by the question (B) Is it (somewhat) more reasonable to apply a Y-scheme to Xs than not to do so?

This is because in such contexts we can *not* answer the question of whether the framework is obviously applicable but must, nonetheless, answer the question of whether it is more reasonable to apply the framework to that (kind of) entity than not to apply it. It is in terms of reasons generated on the consideration of this fourth factor that we can justify an answer to this latter question.

Application of the Above to the Robot Question

It is time now to use these four factors to suggest grounds relevant to the question of whether robots are MPs. As for the first factor: in any case in which a given conceptual scheme has an established range of employment, we assume that the conceptual scheme is *not* patently internally inconsistent. This is the case with our M-theory. Let us consider, then, the other three factors.

Factor II: Is there any behavior, state, etc. of robots which is prima facie explicable in terms of a mentalistic conceptual scheme, i.e., in terms of its being an MP? The answer to this question depends of course on the present state of electronic technology, and therefore, can be expected to change in the coming years. Already, however, all of the solutions to problems which can be generated by the computor incorporated into a robot (what we might call its brain) are prima facie explicable as the solutions derived by an intelligent individual.

Whether, of course, we consider the presentation of a coded

card which when decoded reads as a solution to the problem given the robot to be a case of the robot's solving a problem or simply one of the robot's printing a card in accordance with the input and its circuitry depends upon our ultimate decision whether to apply a mentalistic framework to robots or not. (This cuts against Gunderson's claim that we *can* already apply what he calls "low-powered" mental predicates to robots (cf. his "Cybernetics and Mind-Body Problems", *op cit.*, esp. p. 12), and discussion thereof in Chapter IV.)

There is, then, behavior of robots which, prima facie, is explicable on the assumption that it is an MP. And as technology advances, the increasingly more complex behavior of robots will make it (somewhat) more reasonable to suppose a mentalistic framework to be conceptually appropriate.

Factor III: Is there any reason to suppose that a revision of (some of) the central statements emboding the concepts of our mentalistic conceptual scheme will be required if the scheme is held to be applicable to robots? Consideration of the factor will suggest that a great number of such statements must be altered if we accept robots as MPs.

For, first of all, it has still to be shown that a robot can be so programmed that its actions will be of such a pattern as would be manifest were there certain wants, beliefs, character traits, etc. to be attributed to it. (In a more neutral statement of this point we should replace the phrase 'so programmed that its' by 'presented to us whose'.) This, however, does not yet provide any weight in support of the thesis that robots are not MPs, but merely suggests possible support which could only be generated by a somewhat involved attempt at determining whether the robots which can be made at the present time might have such a pattern of behavior.

Much more important, and more than a programmatic suggestion, is the fact that *many* of the statements concerning the generation, activization, modification, and termination of all wants, beliefs, emotional states, emotions, recollections, judgments, character traits, psychological abnormalities, etc., will have to be *revised*. This of course will effect a great number of the statements embodying many of the concepts of our mentalistic conceptual scheme. It is, therefore, a weighty reason in support of the claim that robots are not MPS.

Why would these statements have to be revised? They would have to be revised because getting a computer to "believe" something is having any key-punch operator (or parallel worker if tapes, etc. are used instead of cards) feed "information" (measured in "bits") into the robot. Unlike beliefs (whether of human or any other animal), the robot's "belief" would, of course, not be "forgotten" just because he has "learned" it long ago and has never used it. To generate a "desire" or a "want", any operator need only feed the appropriate instruction into the robot. Its "desires" would not vary in strength with time nor with failure to obtain their objects. They would only be abandoned on instruction by an operator (either prior to or subsequent to the generation of the "desire" in question).

Furthermore, no factors would hinder "recall" such as long periods of disuse. Its "judgments" would be generated automatically on the basis of stored "information". Its "personality" could be *radically* altered either by "instructions" being fed into it or by a switching of a circuit, as could its "free associations", its patterns of "drawing conclusions"; in short, its logical and emotional patterns could be radically altered by just such simple means. (Compare this with a psychiatrist's attempt to change an extreme recluse into a gregarious person by telling him to change into a gregarious individual.)

It might be countered here that further neurophysiological experimentation will allow for parallel changes to be brought about in human beings, etc., by means similar to those available now in reference to robots, but this is not the present state of affairs, and, importantly, if it ever does obtain, we will be required to change radically our presuppositions about the nature of wants, beliefs, personality traits, etc. We might well have to change the set of statements we assume to delineate central psychological concepts some day to allow for the incorporation of revolutionary discoveries about the human being, etc. That is, however, not to say that in doing so we will not be altering the theoretical framework and its concepts. And insofar as it *does* entail this alteration, we have reasons generated on the basis of the third factor which support the claim that our mentalistic framework is inappropriate to robots, i.e., that robots are not MPs. (Cf. below.)

We can see at this point that it would be essential in a completely adequate defense of this position to show why such a revision would not merely be a change from one M-theory to another M-theory. As stated at the beginning of this chapter, we will not propose grounds for deciding whether what is resultant from such an alteration is another M-theory, or not an M-theory at all. What we say here, then, must remain as merely a preliminary to such a defense.

Notably, the difficulties involved in stating criteria by which to categorize and to individuate such schemes are, it seems, ultimately responsible for the lack of unanimity on the issue of whether such a "mentalistic" understanding of robots is actually mentalistic or only pseudo-mentalistic.

For it is the answer to the question of whether (given types of) robots have different kinds of minds than human beings or have no mind at all that will be in dispute here. Those who counter-argue that the above (and subsequent) considerations are completely compatible with the position that robots literally have a mind (although not a human mind) cannot be adequately answered without an adequate position on categorizing and individuating schemes, which we are *not* providing.

In virtue of this, the final conclusions that (a) such a modified theory is not an M-theory in the case of robots but that (b) a rather similarly modified one *is* an M-theory in the case of humans in an age with much greater neuro- and psychopharmacological knowledge than that of the present time both seem to be, at best, tentative and questionable.

G-Factor IV: Does considering the mentalistic conceptual framework to be applicable to robots provide a classification which is for additional reasons untenable? One unreasonable consequence of assuming robots to be MPs is based on the ethical principle mentioned in the earlier discussion of the fourth factor, viz., that one deserves, prima facie, the same respect, criticisms, acclaim, disdain, etc. for treating a robot in a given way as he does for treating any MP (such as a stray dog) insofar as the respect, etc., is based on the fact that what is being treated in a certain way is an MP. As this is a somewhat minor problem resultant from considering robots to be MPs, we can take it to be more of an anomaly than a weightly reason in support of the claim that robots are not MPs. The anomaly arises, it can be noted, only on the acceptance of the ethical principle in question. I take it that this assumption is rather inoffensive to most, but if not acceptable to the reader, he may reject this from the list of the problematic. (He might perhaps generate parallel anomalies on the basis of other (accepted) principles.)

But this seems rather unhappy. At present it seems rather unreasonable to praise a man because he handles his robot with care, because he talks nicely to it; rather unreasonable, ridiculous to criticize him for talking abusively to it; rather ridiculous to consider him a considerate and socially aware individual because he tells his robot to do only things which he is convinced that it *can* do, and tries to convince others to treat their robots similarly, with respect, etc. Such idiosyncrasy would in general be quite acceptable if harmless, but not especially a moral virtue.

As stated just above, however, I think that the reasons in support of our thesis that robots are not MPs which are generated on consideration of this fourth factor are secondary, in ways made explicit above, to those generated on consideration of the other three factors.

The reasons, then, which have been adduced in the preceding few pages suggest grounds on the basis of which it would be more reasonable (given the present relevant facts) to claim that a mentalistic framework is inapplicable to robots than to claim that it is applicable to them. If, however, the reasons here presented do not establish this, there is no great problem. I assume that robots present a problematic case, and that therefore, it is impossible to provide *overwhelmingly* powerful grounds either for the thesis just supported or for its opposite.

What is important is that we have seen some of the major factors relevant to the establishing of the applicability of a certain conceptual scheme to a given (kind of) entity. This was the major theoretical problem which was to be illuminated in this closing chapter.

BIBLIOGRAPHY

In this bibliography, the date in brackets immediately following the name of the author or the editor is the date of the first publication of the work in the original language, if published. Otherwise it is the date when the work was completed. Different works of an author from the same year are distinguished from one another by lower case letters; thus /1948b/, while different editions or translations of the same work are distinguished from one another by an 'E' followed by Arabic numerals; thus, /1901 E3/.

ANDREW, G., and H. F. HARLOW. /1948/ "Performance of Macaque Monkeys on a Test of the Concept of Generalized Triangularity," *Comparative Psychology Monographs*, vol. 19 (1948).

AUSTIN, J. L., /1946/ "Other Minds," *Proceedings of the Aristotelian Society*, Supplementary Volume 20 (1946), pp. 147-187.

———— /1962/ *Sense and Sensibilia*. Reconstructed from the manuscript notes by G. J. WARNOCK. New York, Oxford University Press, 1964.

AYER, A. J., ed. /1959/ *Logical Positivism*. New York, The Free Press, 1966.

BAIER, Kurt. /1958/ *The Moral Point of View: A Rational Basis of Ethics*. Ithaca, Cornell University Press, 1958.

BARBER, T. X. /1958/ "Hypnosis as Perceptual-Cognitive Restructuring: II. "Post"-Hypnotic Behavior," *Journal of Clinical and Experimental Hypnosis*, vol. 6 (1958), pp. 10-20.

BATESON, Gregory. /1951/ "Information and Codification: A Philosophical Approach," pp. 168-211 in RUESCH, Jurgen and G. BATESON /1951/.

BLACK, Max, ed. /1965/ *Philosophy in America*. Ithaca, Cornell University Press, 1965.

BODEN, Margaret A. /1969/ "Machine Perception," *The Philosophical Quarterly*, vol. 19, No. 74 (January 1969), pp. 33-45.

BRAITHWAITE, R. B. /1932/ "The Nature of Believing," *Proceedings of the Aristotelian Society*, vol. 33 (1932-33), pp. 129-146.

BRANDT, R. B. and J. KIM. /1963/ "Wants as Explanations of Actions," *The Journal of Philosophy,* vol. 60. No. 15 (July 18, 1963), pp. 425-435.

BRENNER, Charles. /1955/ *An Elementary Textbook on Psychoanalysis.* Garden City, N.Y., Doubleday & Co., Inc., 1957.

BUNGE, Mario. /1961/ "The Weight of Simplicity in the Construction and Assaying of Scientific Theories," *Philosophy of Science,* vol. 28 (1961), pp. 120-149.

CARNAP, Rudolph. /1956/ "The Methodological Character of Theoretical Constructs," pp. 38-76 in H. FEIGL and M. SCRIVEN /1956/.

———— /1932/ *The Unity of Science.* Tr. M. BLACK. London, Kegan Paul, Trench, Trubner & Co., Ltd., 1934.

CHISHOLM, Roderick M. /1958/ "Sentences about Believing," pp. 510-520 in H. FEIGL, M. SCRIVEN, and G. MAXWELL /1958/.

CHOMSKY, Noam. /1966/ *Cartesian Linguistics: A Chapter in the History of Rationalist Thought.* New York, Harper & Row, 1966.

———— /1968/ *Language and Mind.* New York, Harcourt, Brace & World, Inc., 1968.

DANTO, A. /1960/ "On Consciousness in Machines," pp. 165-171 in S. HOOK /1960a/.

———— /1963/ "What We Can Do," *The Journal of Philosophy,* vol. 60, No. 15 (July 18, 1963), pp. 435-445.

DESCARTES, R. /1637/ *Discourse on Method.* Trans. L. J. LaFLEUR. New York, The Liberal Arts Press, Inc. 1956.

DEUTSCH, J. A. /1960/ *The Structural Basis of Behavior.* Chicago, University of Chicago Press, 1960.

DEVEREUX, G. /1965/ "Anthropological Data Suggesting Unexplored Unconscious Attitudes toward and in Unwed Mothers," *Archives of Criminal Psychodynamics,* vol. 1 (1965), pp. 564-576.

FEIGL, H. and G. MAXWELL, eds. /1962/ *Minnesota Studies in the Philosophy of Science,* vol. 3. Minneapolis, University of Minnesota Press, 1966.

FEIGL, H and M. SCRIVEN, eds. /1956/ *Minnesota Studies in the Philosophy of Science,* vol. 1. Minneapolis, University of Minnesota Press, 1959.

FEIGL, H. and M. SCRIVEN, and G. MAXWELL, eds. /1958/ *Minnesota Studies in the Philosophy of Science,* vol. 2. Minneapolis, University of Minnesota Press, 1963.

FERENCZI, Sándor. /1913/ "Belief, Disbelief, and Conviction," pp. 437-450 in his *Further Contributions to the Theory and Technique of Psycho-analysis.* Trans. J. I. SUTTIE, *et al.* London, The Hogarth Press, Ltd. and The Institute of Psycho-analysis, 1951.

FIELDS, P. E. /1932/ "Studies in Concept Formation. I: The Development of the Concept of Triangularity by the White Rat," *Comparative Psychology Monographs,* vol. 9 (1932).

FISHBEIN, E., E. PAMPU, and Al. BADOI. /1964/ "L'utilisation de certaines activités de mémorisation dans le cadre de l'épreuve mixte pour la détermination de la fatigue," *Revue roumaine des sciences sociales: Série de psychologie,* vol. 8 (1964), pp. 25-34.

FODOR, Jerry. /1965/ "Explanations in Psychology," pp. 161-179 in M. BLACK /1965/.

FREUD, Anna. /1936/ *The Ego and the Mechanisms of Defense.* Trans. C. BAINES. New York, International Universities Press, Inc., 1966.

FREUD, Sigmund. /1937/ "Analysis Terminable and Interminable" Trans. Joan RIVIERE. Pp. 316-357 in his *Collected Papers,* vol. 5. London, The Hogarth Press and the Institute of Psycho-analysis, 1957.

———— /1908/ "Character and Anal Exoticism" Trans. R. C. McWATTERS. Pp. 45-50 in his *Collected Papers,* vol. 2.

———— /1905/ "Fragment of an Analysis of a Case of Hysteria" Trans. Alix and James STRACHEY. Pp. 13-146 in his *Collected Papers,* vol. 3.

———— /1904/ "Freud's Psycho-analytic Technique" Trans. J. BERNAYS. Pp. 264-271 in his *Collected Papers,* vol. 1.

———— /1896/ "Further Remarks on the Defense Neuro-psychoses" Trans. John RICKMAN. Pp. 155-182 in his *Collected Papers,* vol. 1.

———— /1914/ "On Narcissism: An Introduction" Trans. C. BAINES. Pp. 30-59 in his *Collected Papers,* vol. 4.

———— /1912/ "A Note on the Unconscious in Psycho-analysis" /Written in English/. Pp. 22-29 in his *Collected Papers,* vol. 4.

——————— /1926/ *The Problem of Anxiety.* Trans. H. A. BUNKER. New York, The Psychoanalytic Quarterly Press and W. W. Norton & Co., Inc., 1936.

——————— /1901 E2/ *Psychopathology of Everyday Life.* Trans. A. A. BRILL. New York, Mentor Books, 1964.

——————— /1915a/ "Repression" Trans. C. BAINES. Pp. 84-97 in his *Collected Papers,* vol. 4.

——————— /1901 E3/ *The Standard Edition of the Complete Psychological Works of Freud,* vol. 6. Trans. A. TYSON. London, The Hogarth Press, Ltd., and The Institute of Psycho-analysis, 1963.

——————— /1916/ *The Standard Edition of the Complete Psychological Works of Freud,* vol. 15. Trans. J. STRACHEY, 1963.

——————— /1915b/ "The Unconscious" Trans. C. BAINES. Pp. 98-136 in his *Collected Papers,* vol. 4.

——————— /1901 E1/ *Zur Psychopathologie des Alltagslebens,* vierte Auflage. Berlin, Verlag von S. Karger, 1912.

GASSENDI, P. /1641/ "Letter from P. Gassendi to M. Descartes" (identical with "The Fifth Set of Objections"), pp. 135-203 in *Philosophical Works of Descartes,* vol. 2. Trans. E. S. HALDANE and G. R. T. ROSS. New York, Dover Publications, Inc., 1955.

GEACH, Peter. /1957/ *Mental Acts: Their Content and Their Objects.* London, Routledge & Kegan Paul, 1964.

GINSBERG, Mitchell. /1972?/ "On Behavior and Communication" Forthcoming in the special issue on schizophrenia in *The Human Context.*

——————— /1967/ *Belief: Its Conceptual and Phenomenological Structure.* Doctoral Thesis, University of Michigan, 1967, Department of Philosophy. Microfilm #68-7607.

——————— /1966/ "Katz on Semantic Theory and 'Good'", *The Journal of Philosophy,* vol. 63 (1966), pp. 517-521.

GOLDBERG, Bruce. /1968/ "The Correspondence Hypothesis," *Philosophical Review,* vol. 77, No. 4 (October 1968), pp. 438-454.

GOLDMAN, Alvin I. /1965/ *Action.* Doctoral Thesis, Princeton University, 1965, Department of Philosophy. Microfilm #65-6376.

GOODMAN, Nelson. /1955/ *Fact, Fiction and Forecast*, second edition. Indianapolis, New York, and Kansas City, The Bobbs-Merrill Co., Inc., 1965.

———— /1968/ *Languages of Art, An Approach to a Theory of Symbols.* Indianapolis and New York, The Bobbs-Merrill Co. Inc., 1968.

GUNDERSON, Keith. /1965/ "Cybernetics and Mind-Body Problems," U.C.L.A., Los Angeles, 1965, mimeograph. For an abstract of this article, originally scheduled to appear in the now defunct *Methodos*, see *The Journal of Philosophy*, vol. 62, No. 21 (November 4, 1965), p. 657.

———— /1964/ "The Imitation Game," *Mind*, N. S., vol. 73 (1964), pp. 234-245.

———— /1963/ "Interview with a Robot," *Analysis*, vol. 23 (1963), pp. 126-142.

HAMPSHIRE, Stuart. /1959/ *Thought and Action.* London, Chatto and Windus, 1959.

HARE, R. M. /1952/ *The Language of Morals.* New York, Oxford University Press, 1964.

HARMAN, Gilbert. /1965/ "The Inference to the Best Explanation," *Philosophical Review*, vol. 74, No. 1 (January 1965), pp. 88-95.

HEMPEL, Carl G. /1965/ *Aspects of Scientific Explanation.* New York, The Free Press, 1966.

———— /1952/ *Fundamentals of Concept Formation in Empirical Science.* Chicago, The University of Chicago Press, 1962.

———— /1966/ *Philosophy of Natural Science.* Englewood Cliffs, N.J., Prentice-Hall, Inc., 1966.

———— /1962/ "Rational Action," pp. 5-23 in the *Proceedings and Addresses of the American Philosophical Association*, vol. 25. Yellow Springs, Ohio, Antioch Press, 1962.

HENNINGER, William. /1966/ "The Logical Structure of Unconscious motives," the University of Michigan, Ann Arbor, Mich., 1966, mimeograph.

HILGARD, E. R., L. V. JONES, and S. J. KAPLAN. /1951/ "Conditioned Discrimination as Related to Anxiety," *Journal of Experimental Psychology*, vol. 42 (1951), pp. 94-99.

HINSIE, L. E. and R. J. CAMPBELL, eds. /1940/ *Psychiatric Dictionary.* New York, Oxford University Press, 1960.

HOOK, Sidney, ed. /1960a/ *Dimensions of Mind.* New York, Collier Books, 1961.

——————— /1960b/ "A Pragmatic Note," pp. 184-188 in HOOK /1960a/.

HOSPERS, J. /1953/ *An Introduction to Philosophical Analysis.* Englewood Cliffs, N.J., Prentice-Hall, Inc., 1965.

HUME, David. /1748/ *An Inquiry Concerning Human Understanding.* New York: The Bobbs-Merrill Co. Inc., 1955.

——————— /1739/ *A Treatise of Human Nature.* Oxford, Oxford University Press, 1964.

JAMES, William. /1890/ *The Principles of Psychology,* vol. 2. New York, Henry Holt & Co., 1923.

KAPLAN, Abraham. /1964/ *The Conduct of Inquiry: Methodology for Behavioral Science.* San Francisco, Chandler Publishing Co., 1964.

KRECH, D., and R. S. CRUTCHFIELD. /1948/ *Theory and Problems of Social Psychology.* New York, McGraw-Hill Book Co., Inc., 1948.

KUHN, Thomas S. /1962/ *The Structure of Scientific Revolutions.* Chicago, University of Chicago Press, 1966.

LENNON, John. /1964/ *In His Own Write.* New York, Simon and Schuster, 1964.

LEWIS, C. I. /1955/ *The Ground and Nature of the Right.* New York, Columbia University Press, 1958.

MACE, C. A. /1928/ "Belief," *Proceedings of the Aristotelian Society,* vol. 19 (1928-29), pp. 227-250.

MAIER, N. R. F. /1929/ "Reasoning in White Rats," *Comparative Psychology Monographs,* vol. 6 (1929).

MALCOLM, Norman. /1959/ *Dreaming.* London, Routledge & Kegan Paul, Ltd., 1959.

MILLER, G. A., E. GALANTER, and K. H. PRIBRAM /1960/ *Plans and the Structure of Behavior.* New York, Holt, Rinehart and Winston, Inc., 1960.

MOORE, G. E. /1939/ "Proof of an External World," *Proceedings of the British Academy,* vol. 25 (1939), pp. 273-300.

MUNN, N. L. /1930/ "Pattern and Brightness Discrimination in Racoons," *Journal of Genetic Psychology,* vol. 37 (1930), pp. 3-34.

von NEUMANN, John. /1958/ *The Computer and the Brain.* New Haven, Yale University Press, 1963.

NEURATH, Otto. /1932/ "Protocol Sentences" Trans. G. SCHICK. Pp. 199-208 in A. J. AYER /1959/.

NIETZSCHE, Friedrich. /1886/ *Beyond Good and Evil*. Trans. W. KAUFMANN. New York, Vintage Books, 1966.

NOWELL-SMITH, P. H. /1954/ *Ethics*. London, Penguin Books, Ltd., 1965.

OSGOOD, Charles E. /1953/ *Method and Theory in Experimental Psychology*. New York, Oxford University Press, 1956.

PARSONS, T., and E. A. SHILS, eds. /1951/ *Toward a General Theory of Action*. New York, Harper & Row, Inc., 1965.

PEDERSEN, D. M. /1965/ "Ego Strength and Discrepancy between Conscious and Unconscious Self-Concepts," *Perceptual and Motor Skills*, vol. 20 (1965), 691-692.

PERCEVAL, John. /1838/ *Perceval's Narrative: A Patient's Account of His Psychosis 1830-1832*. G. BATESON, ed. Stanford, Stanford University Press, 1961.

PIAGET, Jean. /1926/ *The Child's Conception of the World*. Trans. J. and A. TOMLINSON. London, Kegan Paul, Trench, Trubner & Co. Ltd., 1929.

PLATO. /n.d./ *Republic*. Trans. Paul SHOREY, in E. HAMILTON and H. CAIRNS, eds. *Plato: The Collected Dialogues*. New York, Random House, Inc., 1964.

PRICE, H. H. /1954/ "Belief and Will," *Proceedings of the Aristotelian Society*, Supplementary Volume 28 (1954), pp. 1-26.

PUTNAM, Hilary. /1962a/ "The Analytic and the Synthetic," pp. 358-397 in H. FEIGL and G. MAXWELL /1962/.

——— /1962b/ "Dreaming and 'Depth Grammar'," pp. 211-235 in R. J. BUTLER, ed. *Analytical Philosophy*. Oxford, Basil Blackwell & Mott, Ltd., 1962.

——— /1960/ "Minds and Machines," pp. 138-164 in S. HOOK /1960a/.

QUINE, W. V. O. /1963/ "On Simple Theories of a Complex World," *Synthèse*, vol. 15 (1963), pp. 103-106.

REIK, Theodore. /1948/ *Listening with the Third Ear: The Inner Experience of a Psychiatrist*. New York, Grove Press, 1948.

RUESCH, Jurgen, and Gregory BATESON. /1951/ *Communication: The Social Matrix of Psychiatry*. New York, W. W. Norton & Co. Inc., 1951.

RUSSELL, Bertrand. /1921/ *The Analysis of Mind*. London, George Allen & Unwin Ltd., 1924.

RYLE, Gilbert. /1949/ *Concept of Mind*. New York, Barnes & Noble, 1962.

SACKETT, E. W. /1913/ "The Canada Porcupine: A study of the Learning Process," *Behavior Monographs*, vol. 2 (1913).

SARTRE, Jean-Paul. /1943/ *Being and Nothingness: An Essay on Phenomenological Ontology*. Trans. H. E. BARNES. New York, Philosophical Library, 1956.

———— /1936/ *The Transcendence of the Ego: An Existentialist Theory of Consciousness*. Trans. F. WILLIAMS and R. KIRPATRICK. New York, The Noonday Press, Inc., 1966.

SAYRE, Kenneth M. /1965/ *Recognition: A Study in the Philosophy of Artificial Intelligence*. Notre Dame, University of Notre Dame Press, 1965.

SCOPENHAUER, Arthur. /1844/ *The World as Will and Representation*, vol. 2. Trans. E. F. J. PAYNE. New York, Dover Publications, Inc., 1966.

SCRIVEN, Michael. /1960/ "The Compleat Robot: A Prolegomena to Androidology," pp. 113-133 in S. HOOK /1960a/.

SIMON, Michael. /1969/ "Could There Be A Conscious Automaton?", *American Philosophical Quarterly*, vol. 6, No. 1 (January 1969), pp. 71-78.

SMITH, K. U. /1934/ "Visual Discrimination in the Cat. II. A Further Study of the Capacity of the Cat for Visual Figure Discrimination," *Journal of Genetic Psychology*, vol. 44 (1934), pp. 301-320.

SOLOMON, Robert Charles. /1967/ *Unconscious Motivation*. Doctoral Thesis, University of Michigan, Department of Philosophy. Microfilm #68-7731.

SPINOZA, Benedict de. /1677/ *Ethics*. Based on the A. H. STIRLING revision of the W. H. WHITE translation, J. GUTMANN, ed. New York, Hafner Publishing Co., 1960.

STOUT, G. F. /1896/ *Analytic Psychology*. London, Swan, Sonnenschein & Co. Ltd., 1896.

SUTHERLAND, N. S. /1963/ "The Shape-discrimination of Stationary Shapes by Octopuses," *The American Journal of Psychology*, vol. 76 (1963), pp. 177-190.

TITCHENER, E. B. /1896/ *An Outline of Psychology*. New York, The Macmillan Co., 1896.

TOLMAN, E. C. /1951/ "A Psychological Model," pp. 279-361 in T. PARSONS and E. A. SHILS /1951/.

TURING, A. M. /1950/ "Computing Machinery and Intelligence," *Mind*, vol. 59 (1950), pp. 433-460.

URMSON, J. O. /1952/ "Parenthetical Verbs," *Mind*, vol. 61 (1952), pp. 480-496.

WATANABE, S. /1960/ "Comments on Key Issues," pp. 134-137 in S. HOOK /1960a/.

WEISS, PAUL. /1960/ "Love in a Machine Age," pp. 177-180 in S. HOOK /1960a/.

WILDMAN, F. S., Jr. /1967/ "A Wine Tour of France, Part I: Introduction," *Gourmet*, vol. 27 (February 1967), pp. 21, 23, 28, 31-34.

WITTGENSTEIN, LUDWIG. /1958/ *The Blue and The Brown Books*. New York, Harper Books, 1965.

———— /1953/ *Philosophical Investigations*. Trans. G. E. M. ANSCOMBE. Oxford, Basil Blackwell, 1963.

———— /1956/ *Remarks on the Foundations of Mathematics*. Trans. G. E. M. ANSCOMBE. London, The Macmillan Co., 1956.

YERKES, R. M. /1928/ "The Mind of the Gorilla. Part III. Memory," *Comparative Psychology Monographs*, vol. 5 (1928-29).

ZIFF, Paul. /1959/ "The Feelings of Robots," *Analysis*, vol. 19 (1959), pp. 64-68.

———— /1965/ "The Simplicity of Other Minds," *The Journal of Philosophy*, vol. 62 (1965), pp. 575-584.

INDEX

Entries are for facilitating quick reference to the text. They are not intended to supplement or clarify it. Illustrative examples will be cited in italics, e.g., *Mayan religious sceptres, Rembrandt.* All other entries of *individuals* will appear in upper case letters, e.g. HUME, NIETZSCHE. Special symbols and abbreviations are listed separately in Part II, below.

161